Unfollow the Leader

Why the Old Rules Are Failing Us, and What Real Leadership Looks Like Now

Reem Borrows

Red Thread Publishing LLC. 2026

Write to **info@redthreadbooks.com** if you are interested in publishing with Red Thread Publishing. Learn more about publications or foreign rights acquisitions of our catalog of books: www.redthreadbooks.com

Ebook ISBN: 979-8-89294-052-8

Paperback ISBN: 979-8-89294-051-1

Hardcover ISBN: 979-8-89294-057-3

Cover Design: Red Thread Designs

TO BOB PROCTOR

July 5, 1934 – February 3, 2022
New York Times Bestselling Author, Thought Leader, Founder of
Proctor Gallagher Institute

To the man who raised the bar
and expected me to clear it.

*I met Bob in 2016, and from the moment I sat across from him, I knew
I had found my role model. What began as a dinner in Toronto turned
into five years of deep mentorship, study, growth, and clarity that
would change the trajectory of my life. Being part of his Inner Circle
was more than a privilege; it was a sacred classroom, where the lessons
were not just about success but about soul.*

*Bob was one of the rare few. A leader who knew himself. He stood
firmly in his values. He didn't claim to be perfect and was willing to
admit when his ego had taken the wheel. He never gave up, not on his
mission, not on people, not on love. And that is what set him apart. He
was generous with his time, his wisdom, his energy, and his belief in
others. He knew pain, and instead of resisting it, he embraced it. He
understood the paradigms that held him back, and somehow, he
transformed his struggles into strengths. That was his superpower.
This book is dedicated to him all the way. His teachings have quietly
shaped the way I think, coach, and lead. Even now, with him no longer*

here in person, his presence continues to guide me in subtle but powerful ways. Not a day passes that I don't ask myself, "What would Bob do? What would Bob say?" And every time I ask, I hear the answer in my heart.

If it weren't for someone dear to me, who shared one email that changed everything, I wouldn't have found myself sitting across from Bob just three months later. That moment lit an even bigger fire in me that has never gone out.

I'll never forget my final Inner Circle session, the one where we were asked to share our deepest dreams and desires. That day, something shifted. That's when this work, my real work, began. That's when I finally connected with my heart and soul. And I've never looked back. Bob's work has not been credited nearly enough for the monumental impact it continues to have worldwide. But I don't think he was ever in it for the credit. He was in it for the legacy, the ripple effect. And if he's watching now, he would not be disappointed. I am forever grateful that our paths crossed. This book carries your fingerprint, Bob. And I will spend the rest of my life paying it forward for what you so generously gave me.

With all my heart,
Reem

Contents

Foreword

You're about to embark on a journey that challenges outdated notions of leadership and invites you to explore the intersection of clarity and courage.

I remember the first time I met Reem. It was in 2016, and she had earned her way into an Inner Circle celebration with Bob Proctor. At the time, I was the executive director of the division within Bob Proctor's company, where Reem had quickly excelled. I was intimately familiar with what each person had done to be in the room that night. And I was intrigued by this newcomer who rose to the top so quickly. By the end of that evening, it was clear to me that we had a true leader at the table. Reem carries a gentle, wise, and powerful presence with her. She projects a calmness that makes others calm. You want to be near her. Why? Because she possesses the rare gift of listening to understand. When you are with Reem, you know she is *with* you.

During the years that I was privileged to work with Reem, I watched her lead with grace, humility, and unwavering clarity. However, it was her conviction, rooted in deep personal values, that set her apart. When Reem approached me to write a foreword for her second book, saying yes was easy because I know she operates with an integrity hard to find. She has mastered what she will show you in this book, which is how to lead with your heart and let your mind be the servant.

It is her style of leadership, shaped through years of study and its application, that has set Reem apart from the crowd. She has a unique ability to guide, not by demanding more but by inviting deeper reflection. Her message isn't about doing more. It's about being more aware, more grounded, more connected. And that begins with self-leadership.

In this book, Reem introduces a robust framework rooted in Health, the Head, and the Heart. She brings together the logic of strategy rooted in emotional intelligence and the often-overlooked need for personal well-being. The result is a holistic approach to leadership that you know is right because you can feel it. You feel the truth in her words and approach.

Take your time with it. Let it sink in. Because what Reem shares here has the power to change not just how you lead, but how you live.

Cory Kelly Proctor
Co-founder of Proctor's Principles

Introduction

The Day You Discover Why You're Here

"The two most important days in your life are the day you are born and the day you find out why."[1]
— Mark Twain

If you are asked,

What keeps you going?

What are you dreaming of? That one dream that forces you out of bed each morning?

What would your answer be? Is it a persistent thought, a restless feeling, or something that stays with you long after the day is over? What is it that drives you forward, even when the path seems unclear? Is it a desire to achieve something meaningful, to create a future that reflects your highest aspirations?

For many of us, this dream is more than just a goal. It's a powerful force that calls us to action. It pulls us out of bed each morning because we believe that what we do matters to us and to the world around us. Our world is often marked by uncertainty and chaos; this drive represents our need for purpose and direction. It's the internal compass that guides us through life's challenges, offering stability when everything else feels unstable.

Yet, for too many of us, that clarity is missing. Instead of feeling motivated and empowered, we find ourselves lost in the day-to-day noise, disconnected from what truly matters. The noise keeps us from pursuing what we want, and we often forget the higher purpose we were striving for in the first place. We go through the motions of our lives, our jobs, responsibilities, and relationships, without ever stopping to ask: *Is this really what I want?* A question that forces us to stop in our tracks and evaluate our lives, our actions, and the decisions we have made.

The Modern Epidemic of Disconnection

According to Gallup's *State of the Global Workplace 2021* report, conducted across 116 countries, employees' feelings of worry, stress, anger, and sadness have been climbing steadily for a decade, reaching unprecedented levels during the COVID-19 pandemic.[2] Stress has become the pandemic behind the pandemic.

It's not just employees feeling the strain. Leaders and business owners face similar struggles. What is it about today's world that has made stress feel like a greater pandemic than COVID-19 itself? Why is it that 97% of people, according to Bob Proctor, remain disconnected from their purpose?[3]

Taking it one step further, in March 2023, Gallup reported that over 67% of employees in Australia and New Zealand were "quiet quitting"[4]. This phenomenon, in which individuals emotionally disengage from their work while remaining physically present, is not merely a symptom of workplace dissatisfaction. It's a reflection of a more profound existential crisis. People are questioning the meaning of their efforts, their jobs, and even their lives. Each moment is spent forcing themselves to do things they don't enjoy. Quiet quitting erodes productivity, team morale, and workplace trust. It creates toxic environments where negativity festers, eroding collaboration and impacting long-term turnover. When we find ourselves battling these challenges, we may feel as if we're caught in an endless loop of trying to fix external issues without realising that the root cause lies within.

At the core of this problem is a lack of clarity and imagination about who we are and what truly drives us. Losing touch with our deeper selves, we risk becoming trapped in routines that drain our energy and potential. Many of us go through life without stopping to ask:

- *Is this the life I want?*
- *Is this job, this relationship, this version of myself what I'm meant to experience?*
- *Or am I stuck in a pattern, too afraid to break free?*

A dream rarely dies, but is often crushed by the weight of comfort, slowly suffocating from a lack of vision and goals. The slow demise of a potential reality is far more painful than a failed attempt. Think about it: how many people do you know who are in jobs that they don't want to be in or that are no longer serving them, but remain stuck in them? What impact do you think this has on their overall psyche? If we never take action, we never learn what breaks us or what holds us together, and our potential fades before it can fully develop.

To tap into your potential, you need environments that challenge you and reveal parts of yourself that you have not yet discovered. Fear and doubt rule much of our behaviour. We allow external expectations to dictate our actions, limiting our potential and stifling ourselves. Stress and doubt weigh on us, keeping us from pursuing our dreams. This creates a perpetual cycle in which the same problems recur, leading us to question our identity, beliefs, and desires.

The questions posed above can only be answered when we take a step back and take control of our lives. There is often a common experience that people who are struggling or stuck in life feel: a sense of losing control. Yet taking the necessary steps to make big changes in their lives can stop them in their tracks.

That is where another question comes in:

If you don't have control over your life, to whom have you relinquished that control?

This question warrants some thought. To whom have you relinquished control? Why?

These questions matter. The answers lie in one word: self-leadership. And that's where strong leadership begins.

The Discipline of Trust

Instead of being forced into different directions by life, we can simply listen to our innermost thoughts and emotions. Self-leadership is the very first step to feeling unstuck.

Discipline is nothing more than self-trust in action. You don't have to be perfect at it or be Number One. In other words, Discipline, in its purest form, is giving yourself a command and doing it.

By setting clear intentions, you free yourself from the grip of stress, worry, and doubt, nudging you toward the steps needed to create what you want in your life, even when those steps seem intimidating or challenging.

Anything of any value that has ever been created had to start with a dream. It may seem effortless for me to have named the business: DREEM Coaching and Consulting. Just throw a "D" in front of my name, "Reem", and voila, you have DREEM.

I had thought deeply about this over many years as I built my career, investment portfolio, family, relationships, and life more broadly. What became clear to me is that nothing of real substance begins without a dream and without hope. We are often told that hope is not a strategy, and that is true. But hope is where strategy begins. The first step is to place the dream clearly on the screen of our minds. Hope gives it shape and direction. From there, strategy can be formed, and only then can disciplined execution follow.

Ultimately, you need to make time to S.T.O.P. and dream, as this will guide your decisions and keep you emotionally connected.

What You Can't Afford to Forget:

1. Pause regularly and reflect on your values.

2. Dreams demand that you develop self-awareness and the ability to guide yourself toward your purpose despite external pressures, circumstances, and fears. Dreaming is free, so why stop yourself?

3. There is a time for action, and there is a time for rest. Know when's what.

Leading with Health, Head, and Heart, Displaying Grace Under Pressure.

We work in a fast, complex, constantly changing world. Today's leaders are expected to juggle a lot, all at once. It's no longer just about setting a smart strategy. It's also about connecting with people emotionally, taking thoughtful risks, and looking after your own well-being while supporting the health of your team and those around you.

These are not "nice to have" skills. They're essential for creating sustainable leadership.

Excelling in just one or two of these areas may not cut it. Those who practise "partial" leadership, focusing solely on short-term results or isolated strengths, may see initial success. Over time, they and their organisations are likely to experience significant setbacks. For a business to succeed, solid frameworks are needed, ones that the company and its team can depend on. One of the most important aspects often overlooked by leaders is physical and mental health and well-being. Leaders who concentrate on strategy without empathy and emotional engagement may alienate their team; neglecting well-being risks burnout, diminished decision-making capacity, and reduced emotional resilience. Over time, this can create a toxic work environment where everyone struggles to perform at their best.

Recently, I met with a friend who had been on our team in the corporate world before starting Dreem Coaching and Consulting. He had been with the same organisation for 20 years and had seen some great times. His career took off, he was successful, and he had been promoted several times into differing leadership roles. Everyone on his team loved him, and he had exceptional client relationships.

Yet over the years, through mergers and acquisitions, he worked so hard and travelled so much that his stress levels were at an all-time high. He felt he was constantly at odds with his senior management team, and eventually, after yet another merger and reshuffle, he was made redundant. It was not until that point that he realised how his overall health had been impacted, and that he was suffering from severe burnout.

Today, a more holistic approach is needed; you can be one of the few who change the game. Something that balances strategy, relationship-building, risk-taking, and the well-being of teams.

The *Health, Head, and Heart (HHH) Dreem Leadership Framework* offers clear steps and guidance for moving beyond your "leadership comfort zone".

It's a crash course in integrating well-being (Health), strategic thinking (Head), empathy, and trust (Heart: The master), creating a foundation for long-term success.

It seems simple, right? How hard can it be to live through the Health, Head and Heart concept?

Picture the simplicity of your morning routine. The smell of freshly brewed coffee, the sun streaming softly through the window, the chirping of birds outside. These are moments we often rush past without giving them any conscious thought.

But what if, one day, that coffee cup remains untouched because the person you once shared it with is no longer there, or you can't drink coffee without assistance? Suddenly, that supposedly mundane ritual is no longer just a cup of coffee; it's a memory of connection, warmth, and love.

Think of the laughter of a loved one or close friend. How often do we brush it off as just another shared joke or conversation? Yet, when time, distance, or loss separates us, we come to realise their laughter was more than just a sound. It was a melody of joy, comfort, and belonging.

Even the mundane familiarity of home holds extraordinary meaning. It's the space where life unfolds, where meals are shared, tears are shed, and laughter is echoed. Yet, it's so easy to overlook this sanctuary of security and love until it's no longer ours.

Sometimes it takes a crushing heartbreak, a health scare, or an unexpected jolt to finally open our eyes. In those moments, the "ordinary" things, like the smell of rain, the taste of a favourite meal, or the beautiful embrace of a loved one, suddenly reveal their incredible value.

But why wait for loss to teach us the preciousness? Why not pause now? Hold your child's hand a little longer. Be present for the people you love. Let the sun warm your skin. Truly listen when someone speaks to you. These small, unassuming moments are life's hidden treasures, always there, waiting to be noticed.

We take so many things for granted and treat them as ordinary when life itself is extraordinary. Why not wake up to these gifts while we still can?

Once we appreciate these moments, we give ourselves the unique opportunity to create a meaningful life. This way of living requires us to reach a place where our happiness is not dictated solely by our external circumstances. When we learn to navigate life with clarity and purpose, and to appreciate the present moment exactly as it is, we truly begin to live.

Recently, I experienced a heart-wrenchingly powerful moment that will be etched in my life forever. Two years ago, I met a part of a family who had just arrived in Australia. From the very beginning, it was clear how much anguish they carried. The father and two eldest children had been travelling for work and study, while the mother and youngest daughter had remained at home in their city.

The father was among the most respected high-end jewellers in the region, with a thriving business and a beautiful home. In a single, unthinkable moment, they had been locked out of their home, stripped of everything they owned, and separated from the rest of their family, due to war. Not only did they lose every material thing they had built, but they also lost the ordinary comfort of being together as a family; the daily hugs were gone, and continents separated them. What should have been a short separation became two years and two weeks of fear, grief, and longing.

The father carried the weight of worry in his eyes; the children were shadowed by the absence of their mother and sister. Every conversation eventually circled back to the same questions: Are they safe today? Do they have enough food? Will we be able to hug and share a meal together again?

Then, against all odds, the day of reunion arrived. After a terrifying two-day journey, the mother and daughter finally boarded a plane to Sydney. When they landed and cleared customs, they walked through the gates to where the rest of the family was waiting. The father ran to his wife and youngest child, tears streaming down his face, body shaking under the release of two anguished years. The eldest daughter clung to her mother and sister with equal desperation, their son standing frozen for a moment before rushing forward into his mother's and younger sister's arms. Embracing each other, they dissolved into a flood of tears, laughter, and relief. In that moment, they were one again.

What I saw was more than joy. It was anguish and love interwoven. It was survival and belonging made visible.

That evening, all five were finally able to sleep under one roof, and in the morning, the husband woke up early to make that first cup of coffee -in- bed for his wife after a long two years.

What we so often dismiss as ordinary... a laugh across a table, a meal cooked together, the warmth of someone's presence... are not small things. They are the treasures of life. They are everything.

That experience became a mirror for what this book is about. It is a call to lead with heart, to reconnect with purpose, and to remember that every decision we make touches the lives of others.

What To Expect From This Book

Unfollow the Leader questions old ideas about leadership and presents a compelling alternative: the Dreem Health, Head, and Heart Framework. This is a holistic model that integrates strategic thinking, emotional intelligence, and personal well-being, with execution for results that stick.

The book is packed with bold ideas and practical tools to help you lead with clarity, resilience, and purpose. It bridges the gap between theory and action, offering real-world insights and step-by-step guidance for human-centred leadership. Here's what you can expect:

- **A Reality Check:** An honest look at why traditional leadership models are no longer enough in fast-paced, high-pressure environments.
- **Behavioural Insights:** Understand the unconscious patterns and psychological traps that keep leaders stuck in cycles of burnout, reactivity, and mediocrity.

- **The Dreem Framework:** Learn a fresh, integrated leadership model designed to help you think clearly, feel deeply, and lead sustainably.
- **Real Stories, Real Lessons:** Candid examples from leaders who've broken free from old paradigms and embraced a more human, resilient, and effective way to lead.
- **Practical Tools:** Guided reflective exercises and day-to-day strategies that go beyond theory and can be applied immediately.
- **Step-by-Step Guides:** Actionable playbooks to help you shift your mindset, rewire your habits, and design a leadership rhythm that works in real life.
- **Three Downloadable Files:** For those who want to delve deeper and bring this to life, complimentary workbooks/worksheets, along with an e-book, are available to help you do so in real time.

Unless we first understand what drives our behaviour and strengthen our self-awareness, organisational frameworks, execution techniques, and strategy models will never work as effectively as they could. If you are in a hurry to get to the *how*, I encourage you to be patient. This book is designed as a toolkit, with each chapter offering a different piece.

Move through the first section with an open mind and give yourself time to reflect. When this foundation is in place, the strategies introduced in later chapters will have far greater impact. Once you have read the book through, you can return to individual chapters as needed, depending on which part of the toolkit is most relevant at that moment.

To lead, you don't have to be perfect or powerful. Being present, being clear, and connecting are essential. You can use all three techniques to lead.

One thing is guaranteed: the book will push you to let go of old ideas about leadership and adopt a new, values-based style that supports both your results and your health, no matter your level of experience as a new or senior leader.

Section One

Foundations of Self-Leadership

Chapter 1

Beyond Survival

"What a man can be, he must be." [1]
— Abraham Maslow

We spend much of our lives trying to survive, paying bills, meeting deadlines, and fulfilling expectations. But survival is not living. Our real journey begins when our basic needs are met, and we start to ask a deeper question: What am I here to become?

Contemporary psychology suggests that human well-being does not come from constant striving or external success, but from three core conditions: a sense of agency over our lives, meaningful connection with others, and the opportunity to grow and contribute. When these are present, people feel engaged and alive. When they are missing, even high-achieving lives can feel empty or exhausting.

This is why leadership and personal growth do not begin with ambition or status. They begin when we move beyond mere coping and start making conscious choices about who we are becoming and how we want to live.

Thriving is not about reaching the top of a hierarchy. It is about living in alignment with our values, our capacity, and our sense of purpose.

SELF-DETERMINATION THEORY

HUMANS' THREE BASIC NEEDS		
Competence	**Autonomy**	**Relatedness**
Be effective in dealing with their environment	Control the course of their lives	Have a close, affectionate relationship with others

The Three Basic Needs. Source: Richard M. Ryan and Edward L. Deci, Self-Determination Theory: Basic Psychological Needs in Motivation, Development, and Wellness, 2017.

Once our basic needs are met, the question changes from how we *survive* to how we *thrive.*

Burnout, stress, and the dread of Monday mornings are far too common these days. Many people spend their work week waiting for Friday afternoon to usher in the weekend, only to feel the dreaded weight of Monday by Sunday afternoon.

After completing my post-graduate degree in Strategic HR and Industrial Relations, I began working– first in printing, and then in recruitment. A few years later, I was offered an exciting promotion that required me to relocate from Brisbane to Melbourne. I was the first recruitment consultant with a university degree to be hired in the company. I was proud, motivated, and eager to contribute.

On my very first day, one of the managers greeted me at the door. We entered the lift alone. Her first words to me were, "*Reem, you may have spent four years at university, but here, it's my way or the highway."*

In that moment, something fundamental shifted.

Over the following months, the conditions that support human well-being eroded. I had no autonomy over how I worked, felt no psychological safety to ask questions, and no sense of connection or support. My competence was constantly undermined. Everything I did was criticised, yet I was given little direction. I worked weekends, arrived early, stayed late, and tried to stay ahead, but nothing was ever enough.

Within four months, my body began to register what my mind was trying to ignore. I woke up each morning feeling nauseous and anxious, dreading the day ahead and counting down to the weekend.

This was not a failure of resilience or effort. It was the predictable outcome of a system that stripped away agency, connection, and the ability to grow. When these conditions are absent, even the most capable and motivated people begin to shut down.

I promised myself I would never, ever go through that again. I quit that job, packed all my belongings into my car and drove to Sydney to follow my dreams. I realised that Life isn't something that happens to me. It's happening for me! And it was up to me to make the change.

Life doesn't have to be a series of unplanned steps. Instead, you can consciously create your own path, learn from past experiences, and move forward with clarity and intention. I believe this was the best experience of my life, and to this day, I am so grateful for it. Because if we don't spend enough time thinking about *what we want*, we will end up experiencing *what we don't want* (the contrast) to lead us back on the right path.

Since that experience, I've learned that whenever I'm in a state of contrast at work or in any other part of my life, I stop and ask myself, "What do I want?" and then course-correct quickly. If you feel stuck, constantly spinning your wheels but never moving forward, perhaps it's time to rethink your approach. You don't have to be living a perpetual Groundhog Day. You can get off the hamster wheel. It wasn't until I stopped, refused to peddle anymore, and took stock of what was going on in my life that I was able to make changes.

Self-determination theory reminds us that once survival is no longer the challenge, the real work begins.[2] The journey toward self-determination is about becoming who we are capable of being, not just existing through routine. That early experience became my reminder that self-leadership is about courage, clarity, and conscious choice, not control.

Conscious choice opens the doorway to greater awareness. When we begin to see how our thoughts, emotions, and behaviours interact, leadership becomes something far more intentional. The following section explores research into why we think, react, and lead as we do.

The Most Fascinating Research

What if I told you that you can do much better? Would you believe me?

Dr Joseph Dispenza once shared, "The brain processes 400 billion bits of information a second, but we are only aware of 2,000 of those".[3]

When you think about this, it's astonishing how much information we are unaware of at any one time. Most of our reality is processed by the subconscious mind, while our conscious mind perceives only a fraction of it. The beliefs we carry, some inherited, some shaped by our environment, have a powerful impact on how we experience the world. But what if a lot of what we believe is distorted? Dispenza went on to say that by the time we reach 35, half of our memories have been shaped and altered by our minds.

This discovery suggests our thinking may not be as reliable as we assume. Many decisions are based on beliefs that aren't even entirely accurate or reflect our internal biases. These outdated ideas and ways of living can keep us stuck in the past, repeating patterns without realising we're caught in them.

If 50% of our memories are distorted, that suggests the data we have stored is at least partially corrupt. So here we are, relying on past experiences to help us navigate life, when all we are doing is creating our present and future with distorted data. This is where the conscious and subconscious mind come into play.

In the 1930s, Dr Thurman Fleet, a pioneer in personal development and psychology, created a simple stick-figure diagram to explain the relationship between our conscious and subconscious minds.[4] Take a look at the diagram below to better understand this interaction.

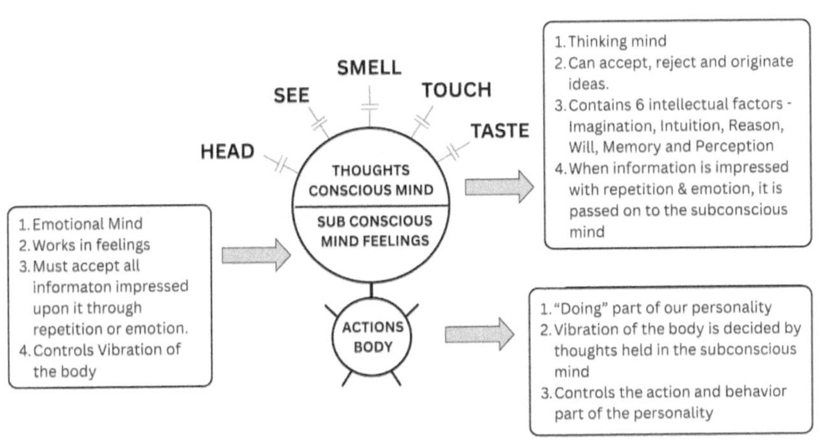

The Stick Person. Source: Bob Proctor, Introducing the Stick Person, 2013.

The subconscious mind shapes our actions, even when we believe our conscious mind is in control. Our body is nothing more than an instrument of the subconscious mind, following its commands based on our feelings.[5]

How we feel drives our behaviour far more than what we consciously think. Most decisions are made at a subconscious level, shaped by emotion rather than logic. The conscious mind handles rational thought, while the subconscious is what the ancient Greeks called the "heart."

We often believe we are acting logically, yet in practice, we respond to feelings. Great marketers and advertisers understand this well. Most purchasing decisions are emotionally driven, which is why effective advertising and sales speak to how people feel, not just what they think. At DREEM, we specialise in ethical sales training, helping people understand what truly drives buying behaviour before focusing on process and effectiveness.

Research suggests that around 96 to 98 per cent of our behaviour operates at a subconscious level, often on autopilot. Our habits, reactions, and daily choices are guided by patterns stored deep beneath conscious awareness.

Conscious reflection requires effort and energy. Since one of the brain's key roles is to conserve energy, it naturally defaults to familiar patterns. This explains why people fall back into old habits and why change feels difficult. Real growth comes from intentionally reshaping subconscious patterns, not from trying to think our way into new behaviour.

When we allow new information to challenge and reshape our beliefs, we grow. When we hold onto outdated patterns and paradigms, even seemingly new experiences repeat the past. Our self-image doesn't evolve, and neither does our behaviour. But when you open yourself to growth, you can move forward and break the loop.

If you want to overcome these constraints, developing a growth mindset can help you rethink and reorganise your mental storage and how you process information. New opportunities will present themselves as you let go of your judgment. When asked, most people, of course, will share that they have a growth mindset. Is there any such thing as always having a growth mindset? At any moment, any of us can fall into the trap of a fixed mindset. It's not our fault; it's how our brains are designed. So you have to catch yourself and be aware of your own thinking and feelings.

Someone operating with a fixed mindset in given situations will see problems as insurmountable and settle for the status quo without questioning it. However, someone with a growth mindset understands that life isn't set in stone and that every problem has a solution. What you need is to be open to entertaining new ideas despite past experiences or a lack of knowledge.

It's much easier to notice when other people have a fixed mindset about a topic than to recognise when we do it ourselves. The easiest way to become aware of this is to notice your thoughts. When you are offered a new way of thinking or point of view, do you immediately hear yourself saying things like "Yes, but you don't understand?" "That is not possible for me?" or "My situation is different." or "Yes, I know that."

If you ever hear yourself thinking these things, you are employing a fixed mindset. You can then quickly adjust your thinking and say to yourself, "I am going to listen and stay open before I accept or reject this new idea". It is as simple as that. You must be aware of your own thoughts and limitations, and always consider what you think and what you say.

How to Redirect Focus

"Success is the progressive realisation of a worthy goal or ideal." - Earl Nightingale

This means success is not a destination, but the journey of consistently taking inspired action and working toward your goals without being attached to the outcomes.

Take a moment to reflect on what *success* means to you.

Success doesn't need to be a battle. It can be found in small moments of clarity, those *aha* moments. Growth happens when we free ourselves from negative thinking, resistance to what is, and the tendency to catastrophise potential situations, and embrace learning from our challenges, gaining clarity about what we want to create.

"In the absence of clearly defined goals, we become strangely loyal

to performing daily trivia until ultimately we become enslaved by it." - Robert Heinlein.

Why do we get trapped in performing daily trivia and imprison ourselves? According to Dr Fred Luskin of Stanford University, we have 60,000 to 90,000 thoughts per day, and 90% of them are repeated day in and day out.[6] If we're not careful, about 80% of those repetitive thoughts will be negative because we lack clearly defined goals. When you don't have a vision of where you want to go, your mind fills the gap with negativity, focusing on what's missing rather than what's achievable.

What kind of life are you creating with the thoughts you allow to occupy your mind? Are these thoughts serving your growth, or are they keeping you stuck? Are you letting your thoughts just happen without conscious effort, or are you redirecting them?

It's not a question of whether we're going to have 60,000 to 90,000 thoughts per day. It's a question of what thoughts you are going to consciously choose each day. Begin with the thoughts you choose to nurture, the images you allow to fill your mind, and the belief that you have the power to influence your future.

One of the most powerful habits you can develop, even while reading this book, is practising self-auditing. This is a lifelong practice if you choose to embrace it. Take a few quiet moments in the morning, afternoon, and evening to check in with your thoughts, feelings, and actions. This simple routine will reveal the patterns that help or hinder you, allowing you to choose your responses consciously rather than operate on autopilot. Throughout this book, we'll explore ways to incorporate self-auditing into your daily rhythm, helping you stay aligned with the person and leader you're continually becoming.

A Simple Self-Auditing Process

1. **Pause** – Take a moment in the morning, afternoon, and evening to stop what you're doing.

2. **Observe** – Notice your current thoughts, feelings, and actions without judging them.
3. **Ask** – "Are these helping me grow or keeping me stuck?"
4. **Adjust** – If they're not helping you, choose one small shift you can make right now.
5. **Record** – Jot down a quick note or keyword to track patterns over time.

Change doesn't have to be something we wait for, nor does it require drastic measures. Often, it's the small habits that make the biggest difference. The way you approach challenges, interact with others, and experience the world completely transforms you. People try to do big things that demand a lot and end up doing them in tiny ways. We try to do too much and end up doing it poorly. Why not focus on doing the small things in big ways to build momentum that will eventually lead to significant leaps? The choice is always yours to make. Will you take the lead or stay a passive observer in your own story?

Chapter 2

Leading Your Health, Head, and Heart

"The whole is greater than the sum of its parts."[1]
— Aristotle

Leadership calls for more than just a sharp mind or a solid strategy. It's about bringing your whole self to the table. Because things are constantly shifting, the most impactful leaders are those who adopt a human-focused, holistic approach that acknowledges the complexity of the people they lead.

That's why the Dreem Triple H (HHH) Framework begins with what matters most: *you*. This focus helps you *integrate your well-being (health), strategic thinking (head), empathy, and trust (heart— the master), creating a foundation for long-term success so you can introduce it across all levels of the organisation.*

Health:

Vitality Over Vanity: Why Energy Is the Ultimate Executive Edge

Your health is not just about exercise or appearance. It is your energy, focus, resilience, and ability to stay calm under pressure. Looking fit alone does not sustain wellbeing. Vitality comes from how you manage your energy, your time, your rest, and your presence across all parts of your life. Health is not a luxury. It is the foundation on which everything else is built.

When an executive coaching engagement begins, the first focus is the person's whole life, not just their role or goals. There is little value in pursuing professional or financial success if it comes at the expense of health, energy, or stability. Sustainable leadership requires a holistic approach, because performance cannot be separated from well-being.

I remember working closely with a manager and mentor for several years, noticing subtle physical signs that something was amiss. At the time, I admired him deeply and benefited greatly from his guidance. Years later, his health declined rapidly while still in his early 50s, leading to major surgery and early semi-retirement. That experience became a wake-up call for me and one of the reasons I left a successful corporate career to focus on human potential and growth.

People who commit to a holistic routine build stamina and strengthen their presence. Leaders who prioritise their own energy and wellbeing with discipline and intention create a ripple effect across their teams and organisations.

This is not about rigidity or adding more pressure. It is about choosing consciousness over autopilot. It means making decisions aligned with who you are becoming, rather than constantly reacting to what feels urgent. Discipline in leadership is not about control. It is about clarity, consistency, and care for yourself and others.

Prioritising health is leadership in action. When you honour your energy, protect your wellbeing, and lead with intention, you model a different kind of success. One that does not burn out to keep up. One of our mantras at Dreem is *Health is Wealth*, leaving us to ask, *"Without our health what joy is there in life?"*

Every conscious choice, from movement to rest to how you begin your mornings, contributes to that ripple effect. You are building habits and shaping a legacy of balance, vitality, and impact. Organisations that genuinely prioritise physical, mental, and emotional wellbeing do not just feel better to work in. They perform better. When well-being is embedded in culture rather than tacked on as an afterthought, teams become more energised, focused, and committed. Morale rises. Collaboration improves. Productivity follows.

Well-being cannot exist only as a list of perks on a company website. It must be lived and aligned with the organisation's deeper goals. Otherwise, it becomes a band-aid over deeper dysfunction.

When leaders struggle to manage stress, prevent burnout, or maintain composure under pressure, the ripple effects spread quickly. Communication suffers. Collaboration weakens. Decision-making becomes impaired. Results follow suit.

The old approach of burning people out and replacing them needs urgent reconsideration. Viewing burnout as a personal weakness, rather than examining leadership behaviours, creates unstable environments and is unsustainable.

Today's leadership is not only about managing the work. It is about honouring the people who do it.

Head:

The Purpose-driven Mindset: Thinking Beyond Your Ego

In the Dreem framework, the Head is about logic, perspective, clarity, and the ability to cut through complexity with confidence. It's where analytical thinking meets curiosity, where strategy meets innovation, where you're able to see the detail and the big picture at the same time.

Those strong in this area reflect rather than react. They pause long enough to ask better questions. They create space for ideas to land. They're comfortable with ambiguity and use it as a playground for creativity.

Sometimes, that looks like a whiteboard filled with wild ideas during a brainstorming session. Other times, it's about listening intently to your team, asking thoughtful questions, and creating a culture where thinking differently is welcomed and expected.

This kind of leadership requires a lifelong commitment to growth in practice. It means staying open, coachable, and willing to learn, whether that's through a new course, a mentor, a podcast, a book, or the hard-earned wisdom of experience.

Early in my career, when I was working in pharmaceutical sales, I had a manager who became a mentor long after we had stopped working together. He said something to me that stuck for decades:

"Become a specialist in what you do."

I have never considered myself naturally gifted at any one thing in particular. What I have always had, though, is a strong appetite to learn. When I was given advice to slow down, focus, and build capability one skill at a time, I took it seriously. I trained myself to listen properly. In meetings and sales calls, I learned to stay present rather than rehearsing what I would say next. I worked on focus, on asking clearer questions, and on understanding what mattered to the person in front of me. Over time, that practice–apply–repeat discipline became one of my greatest strengths.

When I first moved into pharmaceutical sales, I was shy, lacked confidence, and had little experience. I was not a natural salesperson. My manager at the time would come out on the road with me to pharmacy visits and observe. At one point, he asked why I was walking on eggshells in conversations and jokingly started calling me "twinkle toes" because of how cautiously I moved through each interaction.

He watched how I opened conversations, how I responded under pressure, and how I adjusted when things did not land. I began working deliberately on specific skills. How to plan for a call, how to enter a conversation with confidence, how to understand a pharmacy's business model, how to plan a territory for efficiency and how to follow a consistent sales process rather than relying on personality.

I spent evenings building my financial literacy, learning how pharmacies operated, and understanding the commercial realities behind the role. I paid attention to my emotional responses and learned how to regulate nerves, self-doubt, and the urge to please.

Discipline, self-awareness, and emotional intelligence became far more important than trying to be impressive. Despite early scepticism about my potential, I stayed focused on my work. Practise. Apply. Reflect. Repeat. Less than eighteen months later, I was standing on a stage at Universal Studios in Los Angeles, with the Hollywood sign behind me, accepting the Sales Excellence of the Year award.

That's what the Head pillar is really about. It's not about being the smartest person in the room. It's about being the most *committed* to learning, applying, and adapting. It begins with your own growth, then makes room for others to grow as well. When you encourage learning, reward curiosity, and celebrate progress, you create a team that thinks independently, solves problems creatively, and grows alongside the organisation.

Information is everywhere. But wisdom? That comes from consistent action, critical thought, and a willingness to evolve.

How the Unchecked Ego Derails Teams

To succeed, we all need a healthy dose of ego. Along with that healthy dose, we also need an equal dose of humility and self-awareness.

The unchecked ego is one of the most consistent, invisible forces that quietly breaks down teams from the inside. It doesn't necessarily present itself as arrogance. It can show up as defensiveness, resistance to feedback, a need to control, the hiding of mistakes, or the unwillingness to admit them. It can show up when feedback is offered, and the response is an immediate explanation rather than reflection.[2] Intent is clarified, past experience is referenced, and the discomfort of sitting with the feedback is avoided. Nothing is openly rejected, yet nothing truly changes.

It can show up when input is invited, but only as long as it aligns with what has already been decided. Alternative perspectives are met with reasons they will not work or why the timing is wrong. Over time, ideas stop being shared because they are no longer welcomed.

It can also be when there is a need to stay on top of every detail. Work is double-checked, decisions are overridden, and control is held rather than shared. The team becomes cautious and dependent, while responsibility quietly moves upward and momentum slows.

Ego itself is not the enemy. It is the unchecked ego that shifts focus from the mission to the individual. The question moves from "What moves the team forward?" to "How do I protect myself?" When that shift occurs, alignment begins to unravel. Trust weakens. Communication becomes filtered. Progress slows.

Teams don't necessarily fall apart due to technical skill gaps. The unchecked ego is often at the heart of that breakdown.

When leaders operate from unchecked egos, they create environments where people hesitate to speak up, take risks, or challenge ideas. The team starts playing it safe. Creativity and innovation suffer. Accountability turns into blame.

Leadership demands that we notice when our ego is making decisions for us, when we're reacting to protect our pride instead of responding to serve the team. That can only happen when ego takes a back seat to purpose, and when ownership replaces self-protection. In high-performing teams, responsibility is shared, credit is distributed, and growth is prioritised over control. That starts with the leader.

We've seen this play out in high-profile ways. Take Nokia in the early 2000s. At its peak, Nokia led the global mobile market. It had the talent, the resources, and the early technology to compete in the smartphone space. What it didn't have was a culture where truth could be spoken.

Internally, Nokia's leaders created a fear-based environment. Managers avoided delivering bad news. Innovation was stifled by political posturing. Decisions were driven more by internal optics rather than external reality. The ego of leadership insulated the company from hearing what it most needed to hear: that the market was changing fast, and they were behind.

Nokia's failure wasn't due to a lack of intelligence. It may have been due to a lack of humility and a sense of psychological safety.

And ultimately, a lack of leadership willing to place truth above ego. By the time change became non-negotiable, it was too late.

Knowing When to Lead and When to Follow

Leadership isn't always about being out in front.

Strong leaders master the art of being intelligent followers as well. The most powerful leaders never stop following. They know when to lead, and when to lean in, listen, and follow. Being an intelligent follower isn't passive. Putting your ego aside and learning is a conscious, humble, and powerful decision. It means choosing to observe, study, and absorb. You can complete a hundred leadership courses and read all the right books. But this simple truth still stands: to lead well, you must first follow intelligently.

When you're starting to become intentional about learning to follow well, find someone who isn't driven by the unchecked ego, who has traits you admire, and whose values resonate with you. Watch how they enter a room, how they make decisions, and how they stay calm when things get messy. Absorb the qualities that feel aligned. Discard what doesn't. A word of caution here. There is no such thing as a perfect person. We all carry flaws and forms of dysfunction. I learned this the hard way. The higher we place someone on a pedestal, the greater the fall when reality catches up. And when that fall comes, it is unfair to both you and them. We are all human, with strengths and moments of weakness, and it is unreasonable to expect anything else.

Keep this practice going, no matter how high on the corporate ladder you climb or how successful you become. Follow when it is time to learn. Lead when it is time to guide. An intelligent leader holds a clear sense of direction, even when the path is not yet fully formed. There is a quiet confidence that comes from trusting yourself, trusting others, and trusting something larger than the moment.

They also understand something that is often overlooked. If you want to earn more than what you are currently paid, you first have to contribute more than what is expected. The energy you bring is never wasted. It circulates and returns, often in ways you could not have predicted.

It's all rooted in self-awareness. The better you understand yourself, the better you will understand others. When you're intentional about your life, your mindset, and your emotions, you gain the ability to lead people who are still learning how to do the same.

Reflection Exercise: Practise Intelligent Following

Purpose: To develop awareness, humility, and emotional intelligence by observing and learning from others, rather than leading automatically.

How to Practise:

- Take 15 minutes to reflect on who you naturally follow at work or in life.
- Identify the qualities in them that you admire or would like to strengthen in yourself.
- Observe how they:
    - Handle pressure and uncertainty
    - Communicate with clarity and empathy
    - Influence or inspire others
- Throughout the week, practise:
    - Asking more questions before offering answers
    - Listening with genuine curiosity
    - Holding back the need to fix or control
    - Acknowledging others' insight before sharing your own

- Each evening, take a minute to note: *Who did I follow today that helped me grow?*

Tip: Intelligent following is about awareness. It strengthens emotional intelligence and strengthens your ability to lead with empathy and authenticity.

Letting Go of Control: Ego vs Leadership

So many people carry a silent weight on their shoulders. A need to be seen as capable. In control. Doing a great job. Always on top of things.

And expectation is the trap.

Control is not leadership. Control is ego dressed up in a blazer. The tighter you grip control, the less space you create for others to grow. When you stifle initiative and creativity, you end up carrying the weight alone, since no one else gets the chance to step in.

That desire to "do it all" and "know it all" is a fear-based pattern. It comes from needing to prove something, usually to yourself. But having a genuine influence isn't about proving anything. It's about creating the conditions for others to thrive.

Language is another way the ego shows up. If you often find yourself constantly saying "I did this or that" or "my team, my project" in meetings, it is worth paying attention. What is that telling you? And more importantly, how does it make others feel?

When people hear constant use of "I" and "my," it can sound as though credit is being claimed rather than shared. Over time, this erodes trust and a sense of belonging. A team begins to feel invisible, unappreciated, and disconnected. By contrast, when you say "we" and "our", you reinforce that success is collective. The goal is to strike the right balance between taking responsibility and giving others space to contribute. Own your part, but be mindful not let ownership become possession. Choosing inclusive words sends a powerful message: that the work is shared, that people are seen, and that progress belongs to all.

The best leaders are the ones who make others feel powerful. They create enough structure to support productivity while allowing people to bring their own thinking. They can say, "I don't know, what do you think?" without flinching.

The most effective people know when to guide, when to coach, and when to step aside. It also means making decisions grounded in purpose. It asks us to hold high standards without creating fear and to build trust through presence, not perfection. At its core, this kind of leadership is about being aware, accountable, and courageous enough to create space for others to thrive.

There is no need to pretend to have all the answers. Just get better at asking the right questions, listening deeply, and aligning people around a shared vision.

A Moment of Ego (And How To Reframe It)

I was recently sitting at a boardroom table, delivering a strategy session to a well-established board. A topic came up that I cared deeply about. As I began to speak, someone else offered a contrasting view, and it took over the conversation. At that moment, I felt the little voice in my head start to chatter:

"Say something more substantial, Reem. Reclaim the space. They are taking over. Show you know what you are doing and take control."

That was not confidence speaking. It was my ego talking, masked as urgency. It wanted to jump in, to be seen, not necessarily to add value. I felt it immediately, first in my body and then in my thoughts.

As I sat at that boardroom table, I took a breath and reminded myself:

"It is not about being right. It is about getting it right together".

Instead of reacting, I paused. I stayed quiet long enough to notice what was happening internally. I named it to myself without judgment: *this is ego.* I resisted the urge to correct the moment or reclaim control, and let the conversation continue without me. When I spoke again, it was measured and deliberate, not to prove my value, but to add something useful. That pause, however brief, was the difference.

For the most part, I can now catch my ego before it rises fully. When it does, I use a simple check-in: *Is this about contribution, or is this about protection?* That question slows me down enough to choose my response rather than be driven by it. My unchecked ego still shows up, but I have learned to sit with the discomfort rather than act it out.

I am also learning not to judge myself when the ego gets the better of me. Even more importantly, do not judge the judgment. When I notice myself replaying the moment later or criticising how I handled it, I stop and acknowledge the judgement without turning it into self-attack. I remind myself that noticing ego is the work, not a failure of it. Owning the reaction without collapsing into it is how I soften the judgment and move on, rather than carry it with me.

No matter how self-aware we are, the ego will always show up when we least expect it, especially when we care and are passionate. Our work is not to destroy the ego. It is to **notice it, pause, and choose differently**.

Ego-Check Reflection Exercise

The next time you are in a meeting or conversation, pause and ask yourself:

- Am I contributing because it serves the group or because it serves my image?
- What is the outcome I truly want here?
- If I were fully anchored in service and trust, what would I say or do right now?
- What language am I using? Is it inclusive, or is it merely highlighting my hero status?

You will be amazed at how quickly your energy shifts when you take a moment to check in with yourself.

The "You" You Haven't Met Yet – Reinventing Your Self-Image

"What got you here won't get you there." You may have heard this quote from Marshall Goldsmith. It is a truth many people overlook when they set bold, ambitious goals.

Each of us carries two self-images. One is external, the version we present to the world. The other sits quietly beneath the surface, embedded in the subconscious. You might be delivering strong presentations, leading teams, and hitting KPIs, yet if your internal self-image still sees you as not good enough, unworthy, or an imposter, that deeper identity will eventually cap your growth. You can outrun many things, but you can never outrun your internal self-image. The internal picture you hold of who you are quietly determines what feels safe, realistic, or possible. Until that picture changes, it will keep winning.

That inner voice is shaped by years of beliefs, experiences, fear, and conditioning. It decides how far you believe you are allowed to go. When growth begins to challenge that identity, resistance appears.

Self-sabotage is not random. It is the subconscious doing its job, keeping you within familiar boundaries. Getting close to a breakthrough threatens an old identity, and the system pushes back.

This resistance can show up as procrastination. A decision is ready to be made, but action is delayed under the guise of needing more information or better timing. It can appear as perfectionism, where work is endlessly refined because releasing it would require stepping into greater visibility or responsibility.

It can also show up as a distraction. Attention drifts to emails, minor tasks, or issues that suddenly feel urgent, pulling focus away from the work that actually moves things forward. Or it can surface as drama, where tension escalates, and energy is absorbed by conflict while meaningful progress quietly stalls.

"Imposter syndrome" sits within this same pattern. It is the persistent feeling that you are not as capable as others believe, and that eventually you will be found out. This is not a flaw in confidence. It is the internal self-image defending familiar ground.

Change, even positive change, feels like danger to the prehistoric brain (we explore more on the brain in the next chapter). Its role is survival, not growth. When the unfamiliar appears, the message is simple. Stay where it is known, even if it is uncomfortable. That is why growth requires awareness. You must consciously interrupt old programming and choose new patterns before the survival instinct halts progress.

This is also why removing an old habit is never enough. If you want to break a destructive pattern, you must consciously replace it with a productive one. Otherwise, a void is created, and the subconscious will fill it with another familiar behaviour, often just as unhelpful as the one you tried to remove.

Think of someone trying to quit smoking. If the habit of stepping outside every twenty minutes is not consciously replaced, it may be substituted with constant snacking, scrolling, or another automatic behaviour. This is why many people gain weight when they quit smoking. The habit disappears, but the need it was meeting remains.

Now imagine replacing that same interval with something intentional, like returning calls while walking around the block. The habit is rewired to support health and momentum rather than undermine it.

Every step of growth requires this process. What got you here, your current self-image, habits, and identity, may not be enough to take you further. Growth lives in meeting the version of yourself who already operates at the next level.

You do not wait to feel confident or successful before stepping into leadership. You begin by thinking, deciding, and behaving as if you already hold that responsibility. This might mean preparing for strategic conversations before you are formally invited, taking on responsibility beyond your current role, or making decisions with long-term impact in mind rather than seeking immediate approval. Over time, the results catch up with the identity.

Growth does not follow the sequence of having first and becoming later. It works the other way around. First, you choose who you are becoming. Then you act from that place. What you achieve follows.

So ask yourself:

- *When I achieve this goal, how would I be thinking?*
- *How would I be feeling day-to-day?*
- *What decisions would I make with ease?*
- *What actions would that version of me take right now?*

In part, this is why people who go above and beyond *before* the promotion, *before* the pay raise, *before* the recognition are often the ones who succeed in the long run. They're not waiting for the title to start showing up as the one who sets the tone. They're already embodying it before the results show up.

The old mindset of "*I don't get paid for this*" might feel justified, but it's also the one that quietly holds you back from reaching the next level. Leadership isn't about being rewarded *first*. It's about showing your character, your initiative, and your willingness to stretch.

When you take on responsibilities outside your formal job description, for intentional growth, not out of obligation, you're doing two powerful things. First, you're building the skills and mindset for the role you *want*. And second, you're signalling to others that you're already operating at that next level. You're trying on the future version of yourself in a safe space. You get to practise who you're becoming, how you think, how you decide, and how you lead before the stakes are high. This kind of preparation is priceless.

It's not about faking it till you make it, as we often hear people say. It's about doing it until you *are* it.

Exercise: Future You Activation.

This exercise is designed to help you shift your self-image at the level of identity. Rather than focusing only on what you want to *do* or *have*, it invites you to step into the version of yourself already living the life you want to live.

Step 1: Set the Scene

Find a quiet space where you won't be interrupted. Take a few deep breaths, close your eyes, and imagine yourself five or ten years from now. See yourself living with the success, balance, energy, and impact you want. Notice where you are, how you feel, who you are with, and how you carry yourself.

Step 2: Write the Letter

From that place, write a letter from your *Future You* to your current self. In this letter, let your future self speak with clarity and authority, as if they already know the path ahead. Allow them to share:

- **What they let go of** to reach this place (old habits, fears, limiting beliefs, unhealthy attachments).
- **What they came to believe about themselves** (confidence, worth, capability, resilience).
- **What they consistently** did to build momentum (daily practices, routines, choices).
- **What they stopped fearing** (failure, judgment, rejection, not being enough).
- **What they want you to know right now**, to encourage or steady you.
- **What extra mile did they take** when things were

hard, the actions or decisions that made the most significant difference?
- **What decisions did they make** when it mattered most, especially the ones that felt uncomfortable, risky, or quietly defining at the time?

Step 3: Keep it Close

Place this letter somewhere you can easily revisit. Read it whenever doubt creeps in or when you feel stuck.

Why This Works

This is not a "woo-woo" exercise. It is a powerful way to rewire your self-image at the level of identity. By imagining yourself already *being* the person you want to become, you create new neural pathways and strengthen beliefs that support your growth.

Heart:

Real Over Perfect: Having the Guts to Act Based on How You Feel

In the Dreem Framework, the **Heart** pillar focuses on emotional intelligence, helping you to understand, manage, and express your own emotions while remaining attuned to those around you. It's powerful. Because when you lead with your heart, you connect and *build trust.*

Those with strong emotional intelligence are better equipped to navigate the complexities of team dynamics. You notice when someone's energy shifts. You sense when something isn't right, and instead of brushing it aside or hiding behind professionalism, you lean in. You check in. You open the conversation.

Clear, compassionate communication is at the core of meaningful connection. Sharing a vision openly, being honest about expectations, and offering feedback that builds all show genuine care. Just as important is creating space for active listening to understand the intent and emotion behind the words. This is where trust grows, and mutual growth becomes possible.

When inevitable pressure builds or conflicts emerge, those with emotional intelligence don't avoid tough conversations. They approach them with empathy, openness, and a commitment to finding common ground. The focus is on strengthening the relationship so you can move forward together.

At the heart of inclusive leadership, you will find less perfection and control, and more genuine openness to learning how best to support people.

Heart-centred action involves recognising and honouring the richness of different backgrounds, experiences, and perspectives; you invite more insight, more creativity, and ultimately, better decisions.

As mentioned previously, we're only consciously aware of a tiny fraction of what's happening around us at any given moment; around

2,000 bits of information is all we process. Now imagine each person on your team filtering those 2,000 bits through their unique lens.

The beauty of diversity lies in the richness of identity and the broader range of thoughts and ideas. That rich treasury of perspectives is the reason heart-centred leadership makes all the difference.

No House of Cards: Solid Foundations for Real Leaders

The work of Mary Parker Follett, one of the earliest pioneers in organisational behaviour, explores heart-centred leadership.[3] Back in the early 1900s, she was already advocating for coaching, collaboration, and constructive conflict, principles we still haven't fully embraced today. Too many people in organisations are still uncomfortable with conflict or lack the tools to manage differences productively. Coaching remains underutilised, and leaders, especially emerging leaders, aren't consistently given the frameworks or support to turn conflict into creativity.[8]

To lead with heart is to build frameworks that support people, not just systems. To embed coaching for transformation into the culture is to design rhythms that create real conversation, accountability, and growth.

When people show up with empathy, courage, and emotional fluency, they elevate their teams and build organisations that last, with solid foundations rather than a house of cards built on ego and perfectionism.

We will delve further into emotional intelligence and coaching for transformation through the GROW model in later chapters.

Section Two

Goal Setting, Clarity Under Pressure, and Courageous Leadership

Chapter 3

Mission (Very) Possible
Goals That Wake You Up

"Two per cent of the people think; three per cent of the people think they think; and ninety-five per cent of the people would rather die than think."[1]
— George Bernard Shaw

I share this quote in every workshop, training, and keynote. People usually laugh and assume it is exaggerated. It sounds silly to suggest that most of us would rather die than think. Yet, if we are honest, we have all been there at some point.

Unless we are purposefully and consciously activating the creative, reflective part of the brain, the prefrontal cortex, most of us operate on autopilot from the moment we wake up to the moment we fall asleep. Mental chatter should not be confused with real thinking. True thinking requires pause, curiosity, and the willingness to question what feels familiar.

As mentioned earlier, the brain is designed to conserve energy, and creative thinking demands a great deal of it. Historically, that energy was reserved for survival, fighting off danger or responding to a threat. Efficiency kept us alive. Reflection was secondary.

That survival wiring still exists. When the brain senses uncertainty, it defaults to speed and familiarity rather than depth. Thinking slows us down. Autopilot feels safer.

Do you recall the toilet paper shortage in Australian supermarkets when COVID first hit, and lockdowns were announced? News and social media were flooded with footage of people rushing stores, with arguments and even physical clashes breaking out over toilet paper.

We can laugh about it now, but it was a national shortage driven by fear rather than logic. It was a clear example of the brain shifting into survival mode, reacting quickly without pausing to think through the situation. The same pattern shows up at work. How often have we heard someone respond to a question with, "Because we've always done it this way"? In that moment, are we really thinking creatively, or are we avoiding the effort that real thinking requires?

It is often said there are three certainties in life: taxes, death, and change. Taxes are begrudgingly accepted. Death, though uncomfortable, is inevitable. And then there is change, the certainty most people resist with everything they have.

Why? Because change disrupts control and pushes us into the unknown. It forces us to think differently, decide differently, and let go of what once felt safe.

Yet change is constant. It does not ask for permission, nor does it wait for readiness. You either stay ahead of the change curve or get dragged along with it. The choice is simple. Change, or be changed.

So the real question is not whether change will happen. It is whether you will meet it consciously, or let autopilot decide for you.

Why We Fear Change

Neuroscientist Paul D. MacLean developed the Triune Brain model in the 1960s.[2] He found that our brains are formed in layers, with the oldest part being responsible for basic life. This part of the brain, sometimes called the "reptilian brain," helps us move quickly when we feel danger. It doesn't care about your ambitions or dreams. It cares about survival. Anything unfamiliar is perceived as a threat, triggering our fight, flight, or freeze response.

THE BRAIN

A diagram of the brain's evolution. Source: Sumeet Arora, "How Your Reptilian Brain Controls You," Dismantled Mind, 2020.

Then there's the limbic, or mammalian, brain, the part that craves bonding and belonging. It's wired to keep us connected to our "herd" because, historically, being part of a group meant protection, resources, and a better chance of survival. This part of the brain is about connection, as well as the seat of our emotions and long-term memories. It stores the emotional charge of past experiences. The downside? It can make us reluctant to stand out or accept ideas that go against the grain.

When belonging feels threatened, we instinctively move toward compliance and sameness. Groupthink becomes a survival strategy rather than a conscious choice.

We follow the rules without question because our mammalian brain is built to keep us safe, using the comfort of familiarity and the fear of exclusion as survival strategies. As humans, we are born with two innate needs: attachment and authenticity. Human babies are born with brains that are still forming, and so, attachment is critical for survival. We rely entirely on others to be fed, soothed, and kept safe. To stay connected, we learn early that fitting in often feels safer than standing out.

At the same time, we are also born with an instinctive sense of authenticity, a gut feeling that tells us what feels right or wrong long before we can think or speak. This inner knowing is part of how we navigate the world.[3]

When we are young, attachment takes priority. To be loved and looked after, we learn to adapt our behaviour. We learn how to be good, agreeable, quiet, or compliant in ways that preserve connection. This is not a flaw. It is an intelligent survival response. The challenge is that these adaptations can become wired into the subconscious and carried forward into adulthood without question.

The tension between attachment and authenticity does not disappear with age, but it does change. As children, we may not have a choice but to choose attachment over authenticity at first. In adulthood, the capacity to recognise these patterns and relate to them differently becomes possible.[4]

The third part of the brain is the prefrontal cortex, where reasoning, imagination, and creative thinking happen. But under stress, this is the first part of the brain to shut down. Suddenly, you're no longer planning and problem-solving; you're reacting instinctively. Change can feel overwhelming as a result. It literally hijacks your ability to think clearly; as Bernard Shaw claimed, "...95% of people would rather die than think". This beautiful, creative part of the brain needs stillness, time to think without distraction, and energy, along with psychological safety and deliberate pause, so insight can surface, assumptions can be challenged, and new possibilities can be explored rather than defaulting to familiar patterns driven by fear or urgency.[5]

Most of the barriers we face are internal, created by our own fears and resistance. When you realise that fear is your brain's way of protecting you, you can start to question it. Is this fear real, or is it just your brain playing tricks on you? If you're leading a team, think about how this dynamic plays out on a larger scale.

Your team might resist change because they feel unsafe or unsupported, rather than being unwilling. What we need to do is create an environment where change feels less like a threat and more like an opportunity, where people feel safe enough to take risks and embrace failure as part of the process.

What Is It We Fear or Worry About Anyway?

Fear can be a powerful storyteller. According to Lead the Field (2017) and Andy Andrews' The Noticer, 40% of what we worry about will never ever happen.[6] 30% of the things we worry about have already happened and are in the past. Health worries account for 12%, while petty, miscellaneous concerns, like the "he said, she said" sort, account for 10%. Then there are the 4% of our worries that are genuine, but completely outside our control, leaving us with 4% within our control.

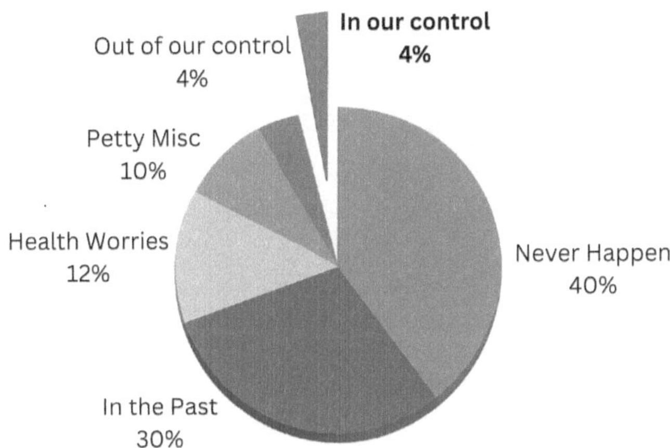

So, we spend 96% of our time worrying about things that will never happen, have already happened, the "he said, she said" type of worries or things that are totally out of our control. By the time we come to focus on the 4% or things that are in our control, we are emotionally exhausted and depleted.

This challenge is real because we spend most of our time fixating on things beyond our control. Yet we know people with a laser-like focus on what's within their control accomplish far more than most. There's nothing extraordinary about them, and it isn't luck that drives their success. They know that by focusing on the 4% they can influence, they consistently get more done and achieve better results. I'm not saying you bury your head in the sand and ignore the problems of this world. You identify the issue, understand the situation, define the desired outcome, identify gaps, and replace nonproductive activities with productive ones. Keep your focus on what you want to create.

What do you worry about or fear? Often, it's not the event itself, but what you imagine it means, like failure, rejection, or being uncomfortable. You might cling to what you know, even if it's no longer serving you, because the unknown feels riskier. The things you fear rarely come to pass, and even when they do, they're often far less catastrophic than you imagined, especially when it comes to our professional life.

When you think about it, fear and resistance waste so much untapped potential. The energy we spend fighting change could be better spent creating, innovating, and growing.

Three Pillars of Purposeful Goal-Setting

A core part of our philosophy at Dreem, as we establish strong mindset foundations, is the belief that we *"...have been gifted with more talent and ability than we'll ever hope to use in our lifetime. Our only job is to develop as much of that talent and ability as we can in this lifetime."* - Steve Bow.

We all make big plans, especially at the start of each year, but somewhere along the way, life happens, motivation fades, and those goals quietly disappear. Setting goals is easy. Sticking to them? That's the hard part. Why does that keep happening?

Not all goals are created equally. Some keep us stuck. Others stretch us just enough. And a few? They light a fire inside us.

Goals are the bridge between where you are and where you want to be, but they only work if they're the right goals, aligned with the changes you want to create in your life.

THE 3 GOAL TYPES

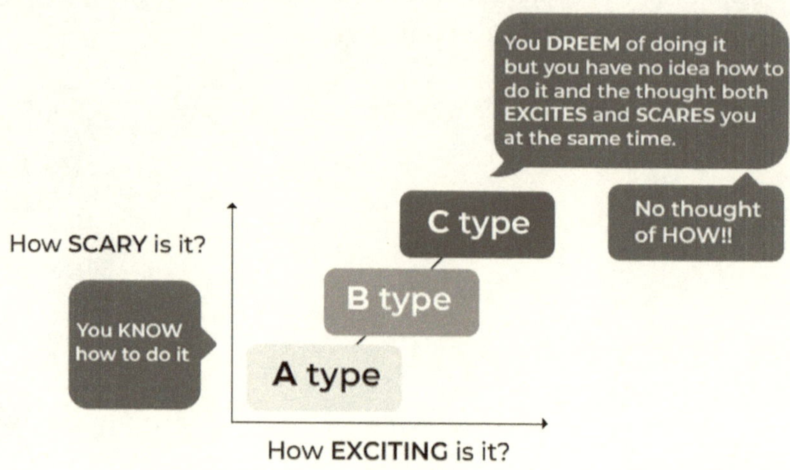

Before we talk about the three types of goals, ask yourself this:

How scary and exciting is your goal? Because that question will determine if it's an A, B, or C type of goal.

A-TYPE GOALS

These are goals you already know how to achieve. They're not exciting, and they don't scare you. If your goal feels dull or uninspiring, you're probably chasing the wrong one.

According to WodGuru Gym Membership Statistics, gyms experience a massive spike in sign-ups in January. Within six months, about 50% of those people stop going, and by 12 months, that figure rises to 80%. Why? Because they chose an A-Type goal, something familiar and not exciting or meaningful. The emotional engagement is largely absent.

B-TYPE GOALS

B-type goals are more ambitious yet still familiar. They stretch you, yet you can see the path. You may not know every step, but you have a reasonable sense of what is required to achieve them. These goals demand effort, discipline, and growth, but they do not fundamentally challenge your sense of identity or capability.

A promotion is a good example. It is exciting and motivating, yet you understand the work involved. You know the skills you need to develop, the performance standards expected, and the behaviours required. It will push you beyond your comfort zone, but not into the unknown.

B-type goals are powerful for building confidence and momentum. They expand what you believe is possible without overwhelming you. However, because they remain within the bounds of what feels achievable, they do not always activate your full potential in the way more expansive goals can.

C-TYPE GOALS

C-Type goals force you to grow. They are big, audacious, and entirely outside your comfort zone. Most people shy away from these because they seem unrealistic. But if a goal doesn't scare you and excite you at the same time, it's not a C-Type goal. These are the bold, scary, and exciting goals, the ones that make your heart race and the ones you have no idea how to get there at the time. The key is to ask yourself: *"Are you willing, and are you able? "* If we go back to having more talent and ability than we will ever hope to use in this lifetime, you can tick the 'able' part. Are you emotionally engaged with the goal? The same questions can be asked of organisations and teams. It's rarely ability that stops organisations from thriving; more often, it's "willingness" and emotional engagement.

So, the next time you set a goal, ask yourself:

- Do I already know how to achieve this?
- Does it excite me?
- Does it scare me in a good way?

A purposeful goal should stretch your belief, challenge your limits, and push you into action.

How to Set Goals That Scare You and Excite You at the Same Time

Setting goals gives you direction, clarity, and focus. If you don't have a clear goal, you are like a ship lost at sea, tossed around by the waves with no idea where you're going. Most people can tell you precisely what they *don't* want but struggle to verbalise what they *do* want. Their dreams aren't clear, so they can't see clearly how to move toward them.

I often joke that we all have the equivalent of PhDs in the art of what we *don't* want, given how much time we spend focusing on what isn't working. We end up falling victim to self-fulfilling prophecies and self-sabotage. This is why focusing on the "what" is critical. Before worrying about *how* you'll achieve your goals, you need to be crystal clear about your purpose (the why) and *what* you want. What does success look like for you? What excites you? What feels a little bit out of reach? If you get bogged down with the *how*, before you define the "why" and the "what", keep repeating this to yourself.

"The <u>how</u> is not my business right now, until I define the <u>what</u>".

The *how* will reveal itself as you take action. But if you don't know the *"what"*, you'll end up treading water.

Take time to reflect on how clarity, or the lack of it, affects your journey. When your goals are clearly defined, you gain a stronger sense of direction in creating the right habits, not only for yourself but also for those around you.

Freddie the Fly: A Lesson in Working Smarter

Freddie the Fly is our Dreem Coaching and Consulting mascot, whose story is based on Price Pritchett's *You2*.[7] Imagine Freddie on a windowsill. On the other side of the glass is everything Freddie has ever wanted: freedom, opportunity, and abundance. Driven by sheer determination, Freddie flaps his wings as hard as he can, harder and harder with each flap, banging against the glass over and over again.

From where you're standing, you can see that his effort is futile. You realise that the harder Freddie flaps his wings and the harder he tries, the more energy he uses and the more likely he is to meet his imminent death. Yet Freddie is so locked into the idea that he keeps trying harder and harder.

In fact, Freddie is trying so hard, so locked in on the idea, that he doesn't even think to stop. Yet if he were to stop for just a nanosecond and look around, Freddie would realise that just five meters away, there's an open door and a clear path to freedom. But Freddie doesn't stop long enough to notice it. He keeps flapping, exhausting himself until he dies.

Now, I'm not saying that we are all going to die for trying harder, but ask yourself:

"How often do I behave like Freddie?"

When faced with challenges, do you think the solution is to work harder, try more, and push through? More often than not, the smartest move isn't to push harder; it's to pause, step back, and look around. That's when you'll notice the open door you couldn't see before.

When I am feeling stuck, I often ask myself:

- *"Am I being Freddie the Fly on the windowsill? "*
- *"Right at this moment, would I rather die than think?"*

That's when I stop, slow things right down, and take deep breaths to help reengage my creative, solutions-focused brain.

Consider how this applies to you and your organisation, whether you're part of a team or leading one. Are you trying to force ineffective solutions when a more straightforward, innovative approach might be available?

Encourage moments of pause. Sometimes, the most effective action isn't action. Step back, reassess, and try a different path, which not only conserves energy but also sparks innovation and creativity.

The Two Key Ingredients for Success: Emotional Management and Consistency

Once you've established your goal, success boils down to two things: emotional management and consistency. Sounds simple, right? But don't let its simplicity fool you. These two elements can either propel you forward or hold you back.

Emotional management involves becoming aware of the feelings that surface as you pursue big, audacious goals and learning to navigate both internal and external challenges. Fear, doubt, frustration, and even excitement can all influence how you act. But emotions are like the weather. They constantly fluctuate. Success comes when you keep moving, by accepting what is and moving through with a calm mind and no judgment.

Consistency, on the other hand, is the unsung hero of success. Consistency is about showing up day after day, even when progress feels slow or results aren't immediate. It's the small, steady steps that lead to significant transformations over time.

The challenge is that when something feels easy to do, it is also easy not to do. Simple actions get skipped, momentum slows, and progress begins to unravel. Remember, success is the progressive realisation of a worthy goal or ideal. That does not mean everything will go to plan or work out as we define it. After setting an audacious goal, we need to take the pressure off outcomes and shift our focus to execution. This means doing the little things in big ways. Consistency is what drives learning, growth, and improvement over time. The small actions, when done consistently, compound into extraordinary results.

During my years working with large sales teams, I found that the most successful salespeople were those who consistently did the small things in big ways. Their operating rhythm was like clockwork, and their customers came to rely on them because consistent action won their trust. Apply that rhythm to any organisation and every area of your life, and you'll be amazed at the results.

When you master both emotional management and consistency, you set yourself up for growth and resilience. You also inspire others around you to adopt the same approach, nurturing a culture of persistence and focus.

Reflection Exercise: Your Daily Practice: Seven Steps to Progress

Here's how to start embracing change and moving toward your goals:
Carve out 30 minutes of quiet time, away from all distractions:

1. Define a big, audacious goal that excites and scares you. Write it in the present tense, as if it's already happened.

If you are finding it hard to work out what you want and to dream big, then start by writing down everything you don't want. Once you write them down, on a new sheet of paper, write what the opposite of each one is.

1. Identify and write six small actions you can take each day to move toward that goal. *Resist the temptation to do more than six actions per day that will lead you towards your goal.*
2. Take five minutes each morning to visualise yourself achieving your goal.
3. Practise pausing. When overwhelmed, stop, breathe, and ask: *"Am I being like Freddie the Fly right now?" "Would I rather die than think right now?"*
4. Reflect weekly on your progress. What's working? What needs adjustment?
5. Stay curious and open. Ask yourself daily: *"What am I not seeing? How could I approach this differently?"*
6. Celebrate small wins—they're stepping stones to bigger achievements. Wins beget wins.

This method of goal-setting will be messy at first, but with practice, you will understand what you need to do. If you are going to *"Dreem beyond borders"*, you need to view life as a journey full of mistakes, lessons, actions, fear, and triumphs.

Strategic Stillness: The Power of Calm Thinking

When I was just fourteen, I learned something I still draw on in times of chaos. My immediate family had recently immigrated to Australia. After spending nine months in Sydney, we moved to Darwin. At the time, we knew little about the region beyond the heat, the humidity, and the crocodiles. What truly shaped me during those years, however, was cyclone season.

In Darwin, cyclones were not distant headlines. They were real and often fierce. Cyclone Tracy had already devastated the city in 1974, well before we arrived, leaving a deep and lasting mark. Each year, during cyclone season, that same threat loomed. But what struck me most was not the violence of a cyclone. It was the eye of the storm.

The eye of a cyclone can stretch between thirty-five and sixty kilometres in circumference. Inside it, the sun shines. There is no wind. Everything is still. The chaos has not disappeared. It simply exists beyond that boundary. As a teenager, and even now, that image has stayed with me. It taught me that clarity and strength are often found at the centre of chaos, not outside it.

Years later, when I feel myself drifting toward the edge of the storm, pulled by stress, urgency, and the world's reactive pace, I pause. I notice. And I gently guide myself back to the centre. Back to calm. It is not always easy, but it is always necessary.

It's about holding stillness for ourselves, and as importantly, creating it for the people around us. Responding from a place of presence, rather than panic.

Your calm is your compass. When everything else feels like it's coming off the rails, it's your energy that realigns the team. It's easy to get swept up in frantic doing when things get demanding. The trick is to build mental calmness through timely action. That kind of presence is not a trait some people are born with. Building calmness of mind with speed of action, rather than the other way around, is a learned skill that requires practice until it becomes your superpower.

People won't do what you say. They'll do what you model. Your team mirrors your energy, your habits, and your emotional tone. You set the strategy, and you set the state. That clarity of mind is what allows strategy to take shape. When you are calm, you see the whole picture rather than just the next move. Strategic thinking allows you to plan with intention, stay ahead of the curve, and align your long-term vision with the day-to-day actions needed to bring it to life.

That is what calm, strategic observation can do. When you slow down enough to see patterns others miss, you move from reacting to anticipating. You connect the dots between changing needs and meaningful opportunity, turn awareness into action, embrace innovation, ask better questions, and willingly explore paths others might overlook. That kind of mindset opens the door to breakthroughs.

Alongside intuition, there's reflection. Reflection on past decisions, both the wins and the lessons, is a game-changer. Success shows you what to double down on. Mistakes? They are not failures. They are feedback. Reflection refines your awareness and sharpens your leadership instincts. The more precise your vision, the more confidently your team will move forward.

Reflective Prompts

Take a moment to answer these questions and get honest about where you are now and where you want to be.

1. Check-In for Presence

- When was the last time I felt calm, clear, and grounded as a leader?
- What usually pulls me out of that state of calm, and what helps me get back there?
- Do I lead with a calm mind and a quick pace, or is it the opposite, where thoughts are chaotic, creating stress and slowing productive action?
- When the pressure's on, how do I react?
- What practices help me return to the centre (e.g., breathwork, movement, boundaries, stillness, reflection, questions)?

2. The HHH Pulse (Health, Head, Heart)

- Rate yourself on a scale from 1 to 10, 1 meaning you're empty and 10 meaning you're strong and in sync:

Element	Rating	Why?
Health (Energy, vitality, physical care)		
Head (Clarity, focus, strategic thinking)		
Heart (Emotional presence, connection, empathy)		

- Where do I feel strongest right now? Where do I need to focus?
- What is one small thing I can change this week in each area?

These questions serve as leadership tools and journal prompts. Real change occurs in modest, steady changes in your daily thoughts, feelings, and behaviours rather than in large jumps.

When your health is in check, your head is clear, and your heart is aligned, you move out of survival mode and thrive.

Chapter 4

The Integrative Approach

The Heart of Leadership -
Emotional Fluency in Practice

"Run with your heart instead of your mind. When you think with your mind, you think of the things you can and can't do. But when you run with your heart, you forget about what you can't do, and you just go out and do it." [1]
— Gerry Lindgren.

We live simultaneously on three levels:

1. As spiritual beings or souls
2. By means of the intellect with the spectacular mind
3. Physically, through the incredible bodywith which we were born

In our physical experience, we are here to delight in life in all its glory, with as much joy as possible. Some of the biggest questions that humankind has ever asked of itself and continues to ask are:

- *What is the meaning of life?*
- *What is my purpose?*

- *What is all this about?*

You may notice some familiar ideas returning here. This is intentional. Real learning does not happen through a single insight, but through thoughtful repetition and contrast over time. Each revisit allows understanding to deepen, shift, and land differently as we grow. This chapter invites you to revisit these ideas, not as repetition but as refinement.

Our one true purpose is to grow and evolve. It is to touch lightly and find our joy. It is to connect to our soul's purpose and live from the inside out. It is to find the calmness to share our gifts and enjoy the love.

The physical plane on which we live, or more simply put, the physical body we inhabit, is nothing more than an instrument of our beautiful, spectacular mind. The body responds to what we think and how we feel. The results we experience, and how we view life itself, depend on the thoughts and emotions we choose to hold.

When you hear phrases such as "you are what you think" or "thoughts become things," pay attention, because that is precisely what is happening. We are masters at manifesting and creating. With every thought and every feeling, we help create our reality.

Isn't it incredible to know that you are the captain of your own ship, and that anything you can imagine and then believe, you can ultimately achieve? The deeper question we must keep asking is this. What are we creating? And why do we continue to create things we do not want, both individually and collectively?

To explore this sense of separateness more deeply, let us look at the first and second planes on which we operate, the intellectual and the spiritual, or in other words, the soul. The mind, at an intellectual level, is a marvellous, miraculous, and beautiful tool, yet it is secondary to the heart. The heart is our gateway to the soul. It is the central chakra that provides balance and connection to oneness. When we tap into the heart, we tap into the Source of everything.

The intellect, or the head, is a true gift. What is required is balance. We do not need to educate the heart. The heart educates us. It is the bridge between the spirit and the body, and the place where understanding moves beyond analysis into wisdom.

My eldest aunt, may she rest in peace, was not an educated woman. She could not read or write, yet she understood life and the heart deeply. I spent many hours in her kitchen while she prepared meals, and she would often say, "Reem, never close your heart," clenching her hand tightly to demonstrate. "Always keep it wide open," she would add, gently opening her palm. "Keeping your heart open will teach you so much about people. You will feel their pain. This is how you learn to treat everyone, including yourself, with respect and dignity."

Stillness is an age-old practice in which we quiet the world outside ourselves and soften the noise of the senses. In stillness, we can return to the heart and, through it, the soul, which connects us to the Source. It is here that the quiet inner voice can be heard, the one that carries clarity, wisdom, and truth.

The intellect is indeed a gift, yet it becomes a stumbling block when it seeks to create difference rather than understanding. Overthinking is one way this occurs. When left unchecked, the intellect can generate chaos, and people can become accustomed to operating within it. Faced with a challenge or stress, the mind may overanalyse outcomes, creating a whirlwind of thoughts and emotions that lead to anxiety, indecision, and paralysis. The choices made here can affect productivity, relationships, and mental health.

The intellect cannot rest. Its nature is to inquire, compare, and seek meaning through separation. In doing so, it often finds itself at odds with the heart. We begin to rely on the senses to rule us, rather than to serve us, allowing the mind to dominate and the heart to recede. Our repeated thoughts, many of them negative, begin to shape how we feel and, in turn, the decisions we make. In this way, a beautiful gift can quietly become our greatest obstacle.

To Be Kind or Right

How do we begin to turn this around? We learn to practise and abide by the heart. When the heart becomes the master, the intellect naturally takes its rightful place as the intelligent servant.

In any given situation, you can pause and ask yourself, *"At a core level, am I operating from love, or from fear, hate, jealousy, resentment?"* Allow that answer to guide your next decision.

Whenever I feel my own heart tighten and notice that I am judging, comparing, feeling jealous, or fearful, I ask myself a deeper question. *"Do I want to argue and be right, knowing it is unlikely to change anyone's mind? Or do I want to understand another perspective and move forward with an open heart? Who am I choosing to be at a core level?"* It is not always easy, but the question remains. Which is more important, to be kind or to be right? And even if I am convinced I am right, how have I helped create a fair and constructive outcome?

Imagine if each of us practised these questions consistently in our daily lives. Over time, we would see fewer destructive arguments, less harm caused by fear-driven reactions, and a gradual softening of conflict, both within ourselves and in how we relate to others. Change at this level always begins individually before it can ever be reflected more broadly.

Many people would argue that this is simply not possible. Life is messy. Situations arise daily that test our patience, values, and capacity to respond with grace. Conflict is inevitable, and our journey through life is rarely smooth. The better question to ask is this. Why do we expect it to be?

By the laws of nature, everything exists alongside its opposite. Where there is good, there is also bad. Where there is an up, there is a down. Joy exists alongside pain. To experience joy, achievement, love, and success, we must also be willing to experience their contrast. This contrast is not a flaw in life. It is the mechanism through which growth occurs.

Yet many people spend their lives trying to avoid what they

perceive as negative experiences at all costs. Ironically, the more we resist what we do not want, the more suffering and hardship we create for ourselves. Acceptance does not mean approval. It means recognising that contrast is part of the human experience, and choosing how we meet it.

Struggle as a Catalyst

Please take a moment to consider this concept and reflect on it. What if we were to change our definition of this contrast between negative and positive perceptions? What if we saw struggle as a learning opportunity, one that provides the growth we need to move closer to the goals we want to achieve?

Think about your own experiences, which you perhaps defined as negative. Did any of them lead to bigger and better things? Could you acknowledge that if one "bad" thing had not happened, you might not be where you are today?

Have you ever been broken-hearted, only to find your true love later? Have you ever been rejected for a promotion or job, only to land a much more desirable role a little while later? How do you feel when you finally achieve what you want? It's pretty sweet, isn't it?

You then realise how strong you have become, how capable you are, and how much you needed that element of contrast to progress in your journey. Shouldn't we embrace the so-called unwanted situations with full faith that the ultimate win will be far more rewarding?

Anyone who has achieved anything significant has also experienced failure and endured some form of pain. The question to ask ourselves is not, *"How do I avoid things not working out and feeling pain?"* It's *"How long do I want to wallow in that pain and turn it into suffering?"*

Mindful Recalibration

Turning pain into suffering happens when we close our hearts and separate ourselves from everything around us. The question is not, *"How do I stay calm and never feel angry, sad, mad, envious, jealous, fearful, or upset?"* Life does not work that way. The real questions are these.

How quickly can I recognise the state I am in and shift it through acceptance and understanding?

How quickly can I reopen my heart? How quickly can I remember to ask, "What would the heart do in this situation?" And how quickly can I recalibrate and respond, rather than react?

Life unfolds in peaks and troughs, in ups and downs. So we are left with an important reflection.

"How could we possibly avoid low points if they are an inevitable part of living? How do we redefine our relationship with difficult times? What energy do we give them when we find ourselves in a so-called trough, and is there another way we might meet those moments?"

No one has ever avoided life's challenges or low points. Teaching this truth early in life would serve us all well. One of the greatest gifts we can offer our children is unconditional love paired with resilience. These form the foundations that support strong character and meaningful leadership. The most adept leaders understand this principle so well that it appears woven into who they are.

We saw this embodied in leaders such as Jacinda Ardern, New Zealand's former Prime Minister. In the aftermath of the Christchurch attacks, she responded with steadiness, empathy, and moral clarity rather than fear or retaliation. She acknowledged grief openly, acted decisively, and held the nation together without hardening or posturing. Her leadership under pressure reflected an inner resilience and emotional regulation that could not be manufactured on the spot.

It is not that such leaders never experienced life's contrasts. Of course they did. They felt anger, discouragement, and doubt, just as we all do. What sets them apart is practice. Over time, they learned to accept difficult emotions, quickly reframe challenging situations, and return their focus to what truly mattered, with clarity and intention.

Resilience: Turning Challenges into Opportunities

Some of my earliest lessons from adversity came when we lived in Haifa. My mother worked in Nazareth with people from all communities, religions, and ethnic backgrounds. I had the incredible opportunity to meet and befriend amazing people who had overcome so many hardships.

While my mother was teaching, I met young children who had lost limbs and eyesight from explosions. One boy I met, Muhammed, had lost his eyesight, the skin around his head, lost one arm, and a leg from the knee down. Despite Muhammad's obvious physical disabilities, he was one of the smartest kids academically, played football like a pro, and was musically gifted at the Durbaki. Muhammad helped shape my attitude towards adversity for the rest of my life. I learned there and then that our adversity need not define us, and that how we respond is our choice.

Mohammad never saw himself as a victim, despite what he had been through. I remember speaking to my mum about this.

She said to me, "Reem, no matter what happens to you in life, always come from a position of strength and never from a position of weakness." In other words, no matter what life throws at you, no matter how hard things get, rise above it and don't play the victim. This memory, my first lesson in leadership, has been etched into my subconscious mind for life.

You can't be the hero and the victim at the same time. You have to choose one or the other.

Years after meeting Muhammad, I learned that he had completed a degree in psychology. He also wrote and published a book of poetry, a reflection of his inner world and all that he'd experienced. His words, his actions, and his strength stayed with me.

Muhammed reminded me that while we don't choose what happens to us, we absolutely get to choose the story we tell about it.

We all feel pain, loss, and sorrow at times. Through rejection, heartbreak, divorce, loss of a loved one, manipulation, unforeseen circumstances, and barriers, of course, there will be hard times, and we will fall. When we fall, however, we need to ask ourselves, *"What role do I want to play in it? How do I want adversity to define me? How long will it take to pick myself up and make this situation count?"*

Going for my first major promotion in the pharmaceutical industry, a managerial role, that lesson came in handy. I'll never forget how badly I wanted that role. Eight of us were competing internally, and it was a gruelling five-stage process: interviews, case-study submissions, presentations, and psychometric testing.

I made it to the final round with just one other candidate. I was hopeful, but I also knew they were a strong competitor. In the end, I wasn't successful, and I was devastated. What made it even harder was that the successful person happened to be my boyfriend at the time. You can imagine how complex that was. I was proud and happy for him, but also deeply disappointed. He felt conflicted too, excited about his win, yet unsure how to comfort me.

In hindsight, what mattered most was how I chose to respond. Yes, I was very disappointed, but I took time to regroup, celebrated my partner's achievement, and showed up at work the next day with professionalism. I refused to play the victim. I reminded myself that my behaviour in that moment would speak louder than my disappointment.

Six months later, that decision paid off. A near-new role was created that was a perfect fit for me, exposing me to every part of the business, and it turned out to be the role that catapulted my career. I know without a doubt that it was how I carried myself, from a place of strength rather than self-pity, that opened that door.

Too often, people rely solely on the mind, data, analysis, and control, while suppressing the wisdom of the heart. Failure to integrate the heart's wisdom leads to decisions that lack empathy, authenticity, trust, and connection.[2] When faced with a challenge, the mind asks: *"How can I fix this?"* The heart asks: *"What's the deeper truth here, and how can I align with it?" "What role do I want to play right now, the hero or the victim?"*

What is required is harmony between the heart and the mind. The heart provides vision, compassion, and emotional wisdom, while the mind strategises and plans the path forward.

When mediating a conflict between two team members, your mind may say, *"Resolve this quickly and move on."* But your heart will prompt deeper questions, like *"What's really causing this tension, and how can we rebuild trust and understanding?"*

You know you are winning when you can integrate the heart and mind, keeping them in balance to make compassionate decisions that inspire loyalty and drive long-term success.[3]

Reflective Exercise: Integrating Heart and Mind

Purpose:

To help you pause, reflect, and consciously lead from a place of balance, where clarity of mind meets the wisdom of the heart.

Reflection:

Find a quiet moment to sit with yourself. Take a few deep breaths and notice how you feel.

Ask yourself:

- Am I playing the hero or the victim in this situation?
- In a recent challenge, did I respond out of love or react out of fear?

- How can I bring greater empathy, patience, or awareness into my next decision?

- What might shift in my relationships, team, or life if I led more from the heart while keeping the mind as a wise guide?

Action:

Write one conscious action you will take this week to integrate both your intellect and your intuition, allowing the heart to guide and the mind to serve.

Intention:

"I choose to lead with both intelligence and compassion, aligning thought with truth and action with love."

Chapter 5

The Iceberg of Leadership
Beneath the Surface

"Emotions can get in the way or get you on the way."[1]
— Mavis Mazhura

Why do emotions matter so much in leadership? Why do we keep returning to them, examining them, and placing them at the centre of how we lead, decide, and relate to others? Because emotions are never absent. They are always present, shaping our behaviour, influencing our decisions, and setting the tone in every interaction, whether we are aware of them or not. Emotional awareness is not about becoming softer or more sentimental. It is about recognising, understanding, and regulating what is already happening beneath the surface, so it does not quietly run the show.

Every action we take stems from one of two fundamental emotions: unconditional **love (faith)** or **fear**. These two forces shape our personal experiences and our professional realities.

All of our thoughts, feelings, and behaviours, whether as individuals or as teams, are influenced by our choice to come from a place of love or fear. This choice resides at a deeply rooted subconscious level, shaped by everything we have been taught and experienced, as well as by generational patterns embedded in our organisational culture and professional identities.

Operating from fear manifests as stress, defensiveness, and a need for control.[2] Fear-driven behaviours are often reactive, restricting growth and eroding trust regardless of our intentions.

Operating from love inspires clarity, growth, and trust. It opens leaders to creativity, new possibilities, and deeper connections.

"Absence of evidence is not evidence of absence."

— *Edzard Ernst*

I used to pride myself on my logical approach to things and would set out to solve problems one step at a time, with a clear plan.

It took me years to understand why Gary, my first manager in the corporate space and a mentor, kept saying to me, "Have faith, Reem." He repeated it so often that it would sometimes annoy me, and I would feel quietly upset, believing he was brushing off my concerns. Gary wanted me to trust my instinct, stop overplanning, and open my heart to possibility. At the time, I assumed he meant blind faith, moving forward without questioning or understanding the details of a situation. It was only later that I understood what he meant by faith was unconditional love. Once that distinction became clear, I could finally work with it.

Faith embodies unconditional love in its purest form and comes alive when we keep our hearts open, no matter what we face. An open heart does not mean we avoid pain or difficulty. It means we allow ourselves to feel fully while remaining true to who we are. Keeping our hearts open is a conscious choice to see possibility, even when circumstances feel challenging. It is the decision to step forward, believing that a way through exists. This is where we stay anchored in our core values, making decisions from alignment rather than self-protection.

When fear takes over, everything shifts. We shut down and

retreat behind defensive behaviours. Instead of opening ourselves to others, we begin to see them as threats. Scarcity thinking takes hold. There is not enough recognition, not enough success, not enough opportunity. From this place, we protect what we believe is ours, often at the expense of connection and collaboration.

Fear encourages us to play small, to hold back, and to control rather than share or expand. It is fuelled by a need for power and dominance, commonly expressed through micromanagement, withholding information, or resistance to collaboration. Decisions made from fear are not oriented toward growth. They are oriented toward survival. And when survival becomes the priority, creativity, trust, and connection are quietly sacrificed.

This shift does not affect individuals alone. It ripples outward into organisations. Teams begin to operate in silos, focused on protecting their own goals and agendas. Communication deteriorates. People become less willing to share ideas or seek input. Fear-based environments require constant self-defence and justification. Over time, this erodes relationships, drains energy, and diminishes the organisation's collective potential. People start playing the game not to lose, rather than working together to win. Ironically, fear of losing creates conditions where no one truly wins.

When we lead from love, the lens changes. Others are seen as allies and collaborators rather than competitors. We trust in the power of shared effort. We step into conversations, relationships, and opportunities with clarity and purpose, knowing that strength is multiplied through connection, not control.

How You See the Workplace

The main reason we experience conflict is because of separateness, greed, and the belief that for one to win, someone else must lose. The "winner takes all" mentality is pervasive in business, relationships, and even global affairs. In organisations, we see this separateness manifest as "silos."

Silos are departments or teams that operate as if they were independent businesses competing with one another, rather than parts of the same company. This competitive dynamic breeds fear and prevents organisations from working toward shared success. Instead of focusing on creating value and driving growth by leveraging each team's skills, people play a game of survival, focused on not losing.

One particular global organisation I worked with taught me about the ripple effects of fear. The team I had joined and was leading had lived in fear day to day for several years, and the negative impact on the team's results was significant.

The organisation was aware of one of the most senior leaders' challenges and their impact on the whole team, but did not address the issues for far too long. This senior Leader had a brilliant mind. For anyone reporting to him, he was by all accounts a great manager. Our organisation at the time was very data-heavy, and he held much of the data, so the whole organisation relied on him sharing it. His reluctance to keep information flowing seemed to give him a sense of power that almost held the rest of the senior leadership team and their teams hostage.

He played the game not to lose, rather than to help us all win, creating a stressful, toxic environment and lacklustre outcomes. The impact of that pressure was felt across the business. Sales had stalled because too much energy was spent on internal battles rather than on customer needs. New products struggled to launch effectively because their pricing was no longer aligned with market demands. The marketing team's initiatives stalled as they waited for approvals that never arrived. Business development also stalled under the same constraints. We were busy, but not effective. Senior leadership team members were replaced one by one as the company sought to address issues in each department. However, the organisation waited years to replace him, and once they did, overall performance improved rapidly. In less than three years, the organisation's culture became among the best in the market, and it gained significant market share as a result.

Those years with the organisation taught me a great deal, and I am very grateful for that opportunity, as it strengthened my resolve to stay true to my values and always act with an open heart. When we keep our hearts rooted in love and act from faith, our outlook changes completely. We view challenges as opportunities, and we trust in the power of collective effort. We don't need all the answers or to control every outcome. Instead, we can step into the unknown, knowing that coming together and being open will provide the answers we seek. Faith reminds us that connection is always stronger than separation.

Operating from faith doesn't mean avoiding conflict or pretending everything is fine; it's not a sign of weakness. Faith requires courage and inner strength to stay true to one's values and resist the pull of toxic behaviour. It involves showing up honestly, trusting that even in moments of pain or uncertainty, there is something valuable to learn.

The Power of Heart-Centred Leadership

Throughout the ages, the world's most visionary leaders have understood that unconditional love leads to oneness and allows abundance to flow naturally, creating conditions where everyone can succeed. There is no need to create an "us or them" dynamic, because the moment we do, the system fractures and everyone ultimately loses.

Every thought gives rise to a feeling. Every feeling drives an action. Every action creates a reaction. This cycle continues relentlessly, whether we consciously choose love or unconsciously operate from fear.

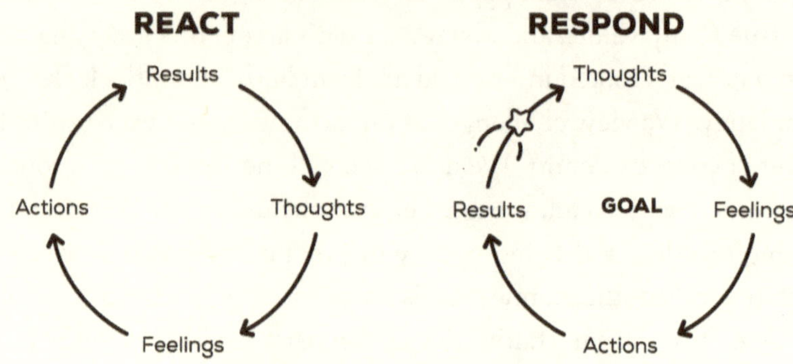

The React vs. Respond Model. Source: Proctor Gallagher Institute, Thinking into Results, 2010

In every situation, we have a choice. We can react, or we can respond.[3] Consider the cycle set in motion by each option in the React Respond Model pictured.

Reacting is usually automatic. A trigger appears, and emotion takes over, often leading to frustration, stress, or defensiveness. From this place, communication breaks down, regret can follow, conflict escalates, and familiar patterns repeat without producing positive outcomes for anyone.

Responding introduces a pause. A considered response invites us to breathe, reflect, and choose how we want to act. That brief pause creates clarity, composure, and presence. In the workplace, reacting under pressure often results in short-term fixes, blame, and decisions driven by habit. Responding, on the other hand, creates space to ask better questions, involve others, explore different perspectives, and interrupt the cycle of doing the same things while expecting different results.

Choosing to respond rather than react is one of the most powerful decisions we can make. It strengthens emotional awareness, deepens relationships, and supports a leadership style that creates lasting change.

When you find yourself at this crossroads, pause. Take a breath and ask one simple, grounding question. *"What do I want the outcome of this situation to be?"* From that place, visualise the end result, then choose thoughts, feelings, and actions that align with it.

How the Subconscious Mind Affects Organisational Behaviour

Let's lean further into the research suggesting we have 60,000 to 90,000 thoughts per day, with as many as 90% of them repeated daily. Within organisations, repetitive thoughts shape habits, behaviours, and, ultimately, paradigms guide how teams communicate, collaborate, and solve problems. These paradigms operate at a subconscious level, driving 96-98% of our behaviour.[4] Left unchecked, these habitual patterns can create cycles of fear, resistance, and stagnation.

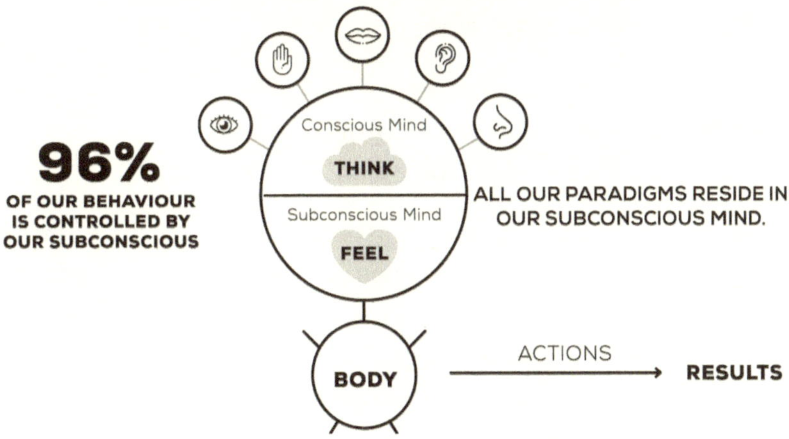

The Stick Person Model of the Mind. Source: Dr. Thurman Fleet (1934); popularized by Bob Proctor and Proctor Gallagher Institute.

Paradigms form through two primary methods: constant spaced repetition or emotional impact. The key is to understand that these paradigms are not fixed; they can be consciously reshaped through deliberate effort.

How Fear-Based Patterns Are Reinforced

The human mind processes information in images, whether recalling the past, imagining the future, or processing the present. The subconscious mind cannot differentiate between reality and imagination, which means the stories we tell ourselves about our colleagues, our work environment, or our capabilities, shape our behaviour and, in turn, our reality. If organisations repeatedly reinforce fear-based narratives, such as "failure is not an option" or "we've always done it this way," they create paradigms that limit growth and perpetuate dysfunction. Similarly, the "Big Lie Theory" suggests that if a falsehood is repeated often enough, it becomes accepted as truth. In organisations, this could manifest as beliefs such as "our department is the only one that delivers results" or "collaboration slows us down". These narratives, when left unchallenged, create division, inefficiency, and resistance to change.

The Iceberg of Organisational Culture: Understanding Behaviour

Imagine organisational behaviour as an iceberg. Above the surface are the observable behaviours and outcomes shaped by these underlying emotions. But below the surface, the underlying emotions and paradigms run deep. When fear dominates, you see micromanagement, siloed decision-making, and disengagement. When heart-centred leadership prevails, you see trust, collaboration, and innovation.

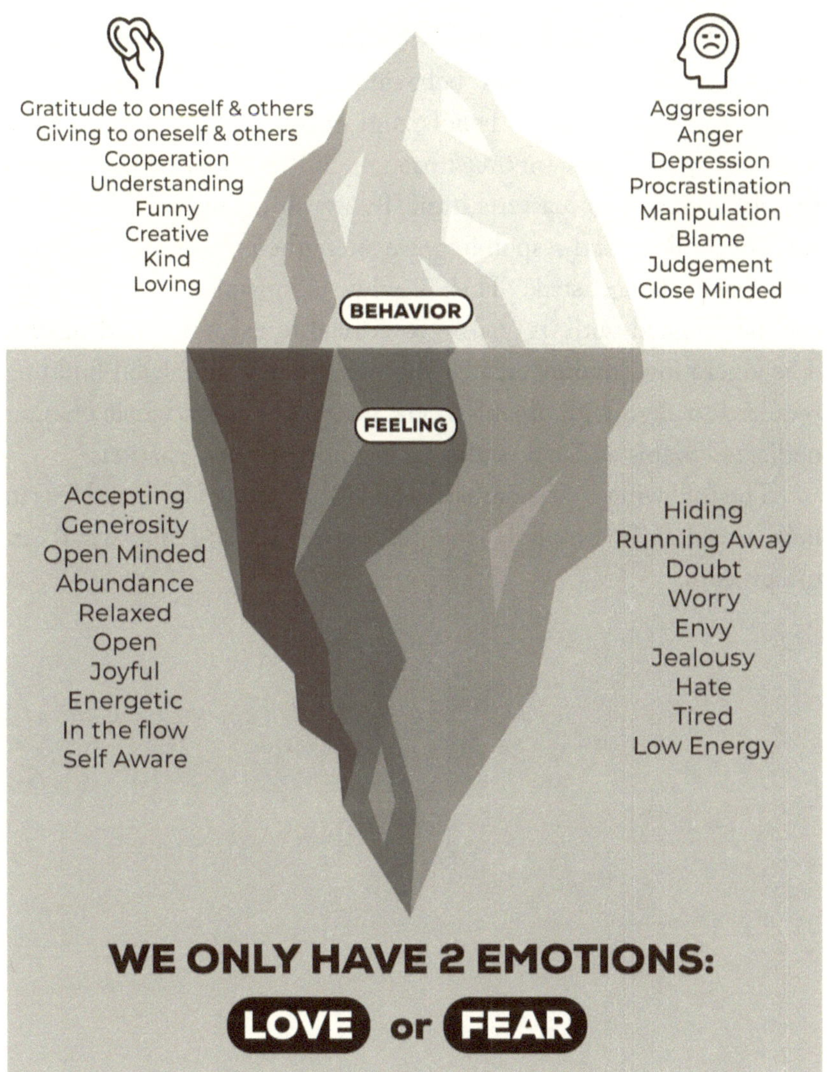

The Iceberg Model. Source: Dream Coaching and Consulting PTY LTD, 2020.

The key to transforming culture is addressing what lies beneath the surface. We often look only at behaviour on the surface, without understanding its origins. By addressing the entire iceberg, people gain insight into what drives their behaviour, and that awareness can spark rapid change.

Word of caution: Sustaining this change takes constant, spaced repetition. Because human behaviour is so deeply conditioned, shaped by years of habits, beliefs, and unconscious patterns, awareness may spark an instant breakthrough. Still, without reinforcement, the old wiring soon reasserts itself. By revisiting and practising new ways of thinking and responding, we strengthen the neural pathways that make change stick. This is why an organisation's operating rhythm, aligned with its goal, is so critical to execution and results. The operating rhythm creates the consistency and habit-building required to align with organisational goals. There is a whole chapter dedicated to this with a downloadable guide in a later chapter.

The following chart compares the visible signs of faith and fear to help us identify not only the tip of the iceberg but what lies underneath.

LOVE	FEAR
Joyful	Melancholic
Giving to oneself and others	Jealous
Grateful for oneself and others	Resentful
Cooperative	Envious
Understanding oneself and others	Manipulative
Open	Low on energy
Adventurous	Blaming
Restful	Anxious
Funny	Humourless
Creative	Closed-minded

In the flow	Scared
Relaxed	Stressed
Energetic	Worried
Caring	Procrastinating
Kind to oneself and others	Perfectionist
Abundant	Addicted
Prosperous	Lacking
Loving oneself and others	Aggressive
Accepting oneself and others	Judgmental

We have the power to rewrite the story in our organisations. By asking questions like, *"Am I operating from a place of abundance or scarcity?"* or *"What impact will this decision have on trust and connection?"* we can shift our focus from self-preservation to collective success.

When you choose heart-centred leadership, you model behaviours that inspire others, creating a ripple effect throughout the organisation. It cannot be stressed enough: *Choosing love doesn't mean avoiding conflict or difficult conversations. It means approaching them with empathy, curiosity, and a genuine desire for mutual growth.*

Challenging Paradigms and Encouraging Growth

Breaking fear-based cycles requires curiosity and openness. Growth often begins when we are willing to question our assumptions, explore new perspectives, and lean into discomfort. No one is perfect. We all make mistakes during times of stress, pressure, or crisis. Even after years of building awareness and striving to lead in a heart-centred way, I have still missed the mark at times. I'll never forget one particular senior leadership training when the same Senior Leader mentioned earlier triggered one of my subconscious fears. I reacted with so much anger in front of the entire Senior Leadership team. The Regional Head followed up with a private conversation to explain the impact of my behaviour on my long-term relationship with colleagues.

In that moment, I was taken aback. I felt the urge to defend myself (My Ego trying to protect me). Bad behaviour from this particular Senior Leader had long been tolerated. Yet, the one time I "lost it" (admittedly, quite badly), I was pulled up and told it would damage my corporate image. With time, though, I came to understand why the feedback mattered. People can grow used to ongoing poor behaviour, but when someone who is usually calm and measured loses control even once, that incident is what others remember. Is it fair? No. Was the feedback valuable? Absolutely.

Ultimately, the choice between love and fear is more than a personal one; it is a strategic decision that shapes an organisation's culture, success, and legacy. By choosing love, openness, trust, and connection, we can create environments where everyone feels valued, empowered, and inspired to achieve their best.

The Quality of Your Leadership is Determined by the Quality of the Questions You Ask

If, as Dr Joe Dispenza suggests, the brain handles 400 billion bits of information every second, but we consciously only register 2,000, how reliable is our perception of reality? How can we ever be certain we are right? How can we speak in absolutes? If most of our thoughts and decisions are shaped by what lies beyond our conscious awareness, the most powerful way to expand our view is to question our perceptions with curiosity and a genuine desire to grow.

Powerful questions serve as a bridge between the unconscious and the conscious. They bring clarity, challenge assumptions, and unlock creative solutions. When you ask open-ended, high-quality questions of yourself and your team, you drive transformation. Asking quality, open-ended questions is what will determine our success. New solutions only come from asking the right questions and moving away from absolutes, where everything is set in stone.

What fresh questions could we ask ourselves to open up new possibilities, uncover hidden perspectives, and discover better ways of doing things? The questions you ask set the tone for the outcomes you create. Asking *"Who is to blame for this mistake?"* shifts attention away from solutions and creates a culture of fear. In contrast, when you ask, *"What can I/we learn from this experience, and how can I/we improve?"* you create a culture of trust, collaboration, and growth. Asking, *"Why can't you meet your targets?"* or *"What is wrong with this team?"* instils defensiveness and erodes morale. With a growth-oriented mindset, you can reframe the situation by asking: *"What obstacles are we facing, and how can I better support you in overcoming them?"*

In moments of self-doubt, the questions you ask yourself are equally transformative. When faced with challenges, you could ask:

· *Why does this always happen to me?* (limiting)

· *What is this experience teaching me? How can I use this to grow?* (empowering)

By reframing your questions, you shift your mindset from self-blame to self-discovery, and from limitation to possibility.

The table below illustrates the difference between operating from love versus fear in the questions you ask:

When Operating with Love	When Operating with Fear
"What opportunities can we explore here?"	*"Who's responsible for this failure?"*
"How can I better support my team?"	*"Why can't you get this right?"*
"Who can help me see this differently?"	*"What if people think I am not good enough?"*
"What's the root cause, and how can we solve it?"	*"What's wrong with this team?"*

Thoughtful questions invite self-awareness, build trust, and open the door to growth, even in challenging moments. By asking the right questions, we learn to become the source rather than the seeker, pausing long enough to recognise that, more often than not, the answers already exist within us. And when they do not, thoughtful questioning guides us toward the right conversations and the people who can help, allowing insight to emerge through connection rather than force.

Coaching for Transformation: From Seeker to Source

Organisational success depends on two more essential elements:

- Constructive conflict, where differences of opinion are valued, not feared.
- Coaching for transformation, where powerful questions and structured reflection drive awareness, growth, and accountability.

When these two forces coexist within a healthy operating rhythm, everything begins to change. Meetings become spaces for shared discovery rather than directive control. Feedback becomes an act of growth rather than criticism. Leaders become enablers of insight rather than keepers of answers.

People in most workplaces have been conditioned to bring their problems to their managers, expecting them to provide answers. While this might feel efficient in the short term, it slowly builds dependency and limits growth. Leadership is about creating the space for others to discover their solutions.

Coaching for transformation is not a soft skill or a nice-to-have. It is a critical leadership discipline that drives accountability, innovation, and performance. When embedded into the organisational rhythm, coaching becomes the heartbeat of a learning culture. Over time, it forms part of the organisation's DNA, shaping how people think, communicate, and make decisions.

At its essence, coaching is about asking purposeful, open-ended questions that expand awareness and unlock potential. True coaching creates self-reliance, not reliance on the leader. It helps people see possibilities they could not see before, transforming both mindset and behaviour. Yet this takes conscious practice. When things get busy, the habit of "telling" can become the default. It feels faster and easier in the moment, but it often limits growth in the long term.

One of the most enduring and widely adopted coaching frameworks is the GROW Model, developed in the 1980s by Sir John Whitmore and his colleagues Graham Alexander and Alan Fine. Rooted in the principles of human potential and sports psychology, the GROW model offered a clear, practical framework for coaching conversations that drive performance and personal development. Over time, many variations have emerged, including TGROW (adding Topic), OSKAR (Outcome, Scaling, Know-how, Affirm, Review), and CLEAR (Contracting, Listening, Exploring, Action, Review). Yet the simplicity and adaptability of GROW remain its greatest strength.

GROW stands for:

- Goal: What outcome do we want to achieve?
- Reality: What is happening right now? What is the truth beneath the surface?
- Options: What choices and opportunities exist?
- Will: What commitment will you make to move forward?

When used effectively, GROW transforms problem-focused discussions into growth-focused dialogues. It moves people from seeking solutions from others to becoming the source of their own insight. Imagine if every leader consistently integrated coaching questions into their operating rhythm through weekly check-ins, project reviews, or performance conversations. Over time, the cumulative impact would reshape culture itself. People would start leading themselves. Instead of dependency, you would see distributed accountability. Instead of silence or compliance, you would see engagement and curiosity.

Coaching for transformation also encourages constructive conflict, which is the healthy exchange of diverse perspectives that sparks innovation. When leaders coach, they create a psychological safety that invites differences rather than avoiding them. Constructive conflict and transformational coaching work hand in hand. One challenges thinking, and the other expands it. Constructive conflict interrupts habitual patterns and brings unspoken assumptions into the open. It asks people to articulate why they think the way they do, to listen to perspectives that differ from their own, and to sit with the discomfort that often arises when familiar ideas are questioned. This process stretches thinking beyond what is known or comfortable, preventing teams from defaulting to consensus, compliance, or surface-level agreement.

Coaching expands thinking by creating conditions that allow people to stay present with that discomfort. Transformational coaching helps individuals regulate their emotional responses, separate ideas from identity, and remain curious rather than defensive. It encourages reflection rather than reaction and helps people examine their own thinking without feeling threatened or diminished. In this space, insight can emerge because they are supported to think more deeply and more broadly, rather than being told what to think.

Together, constructive conflict and transformational coaching enable teams to engage with tension in a healthy and productive way. Rather than avoiding difficult conversations or becoming polarised by them, teams learn to navigate disagreement with maturity and respect. Under pressure, they are less likely to revert to control, blame, or old habits and more able to adapt intentionally. Diverse viewpoints are no longer seen as obstacles to progress but as valuable inputs that sharpen decision-making, strengthen relationships, and support sustained progress over time.

To bring this to life in your own organisation, you can visit **dreem.com.au/lead-differently** to download our GROW Coaching Model and Framework. This practical guide will help you embed solution-based conversations into your leadership rhythm, empowering your team to think deeply, take ownership, and grow through every challenge.

Coaching is the bridge between awareness and action. It is the practice that transforms knowledge into wisdom and intention into impact. Take a moment to reflect on how you can bring this mindset into your leadership rhythm. The questions you ask, and the space you create for others to find their own answers, will determine not only your success but also the legacy you leave as a leader.

Reflective Exercise: Leadership in Practice - Coaching Beneath the Surface

Purpose:

To help you bring emotional awareness, heart-centred decision-making, and a coaching mindset into daily leadership practice - leading from faith, not fear.

Reflection:

Take a quiet moment to reflect on a recent situation with your team or peers.

Ask yourself:

- Was I leading from love and trust, or reacting from fear and control?
- What emotions or assumptions might have been driving my response beneath the surface?
- Did I give others the space to think, reflect, and grow? Or did I jump in with the answer?
- What questions could I have asked to help them uncover their own solutions?

Action:

Choose one upcoming conversation where you will practise coaching through the GROW model:

- Goal: What outcome are we working towards?
- Reality: What is happening right now?
- Options: What could we try?
- Will: What will you commit to doing next?

Intention:

Coaching Mantra: "*I create space for growth through heart-centred leadership, asking powerful questions, and trusting the process. True leadership is not found in having the answers, but in helping others discover their own.*"

Many people mistake heart-centred leadership and unconditional love for weakness, but love is not weak. Leading from the heart requires an enormous amount of inner strength. Anger is easy. Division is easy. Conflict is easy. Ghosting people is easy. Love requires you to drop the self-protective ego, to drop all blame, to be true to your values, and to focus solely on what's within your control. Heart-centred leadership brings purpose and requires an inordinate amount of honesty and continuous work.

Understanding and managing your emotions creates significant change. Your leadership becomes clear, connected, and present. Emotional fluency in action is the very definition of bravery, as is the ability to know and understand your own emotions and others'.

Chapter 6

The Courage to Lead

Transforming Fear into
Connection, Resilience, and Legacy

A leader is one who knows the way, goes the way, and shows the way."[1]
—John C. Maxwell

The Elephant in the Room: Seeing the Bigger Picture

Buddha's story of the blind men and the elephant is a profound lesson in the dangers of partial perspectives.

Once, in a dense forest, there were four blind men who had never seen an elephant before. They were curious about this magnificent creature, so they decided to visit a nearby village where an elephant resided to learn about it. The villagers led the blind men to the elephant and allowed them to touch and feel the animal so they could understand its true nature.

The first blind man touched the elephant's side and said, "An elephant is like a great, sturdy wall." The second blind man felt the elephant's tusk and declared, "No, an elephant is like a sharp, pointed spear." The third blind man grasped the elephant's trunk, and he was certain that the elephant resembled a thick, writhing snake. Finally, the fourth blind man touched the elephant's leg and proclaimed, "You are all wrong. An elephant is like a strong, tall tree."

Each of the blind men believed that their individual experience and understanding of the elephant represented the whole truth. They argued and insisted that their perspective was the only correct one. The villagers, who could see the entire elephant, recognised that each of the blind men was only partially right. In reality, the elephant was much greater and more complex than any one of them could perceive.

Buddha then went on to explain, "Just like the blind men and the elephant, people often perceive only a fragment of reality while believing that their limited understanding represents the entire truth. They cling to their separate experiences, failing to recognise that everything in the world is interconnected, and any notion of separation is an illusion."

Much like these blind men, it's easy for any of us to base decisions on incomplete information, reacting to immediate symptoms without understanding the broader context.

Real progress is not about quick fixes. It's about understanding, reflection, empathy and courage. The courage to dive beneath the surface and address the root cause of challenges rather than simply masking their symptoms. Too often, teams and organisations find themselves firefighting by introducing stricter deadlines, more detailed metrics, or one more meeting to address an issue. But what if we stopped to ask *"What's really going on here?"*

What if, instead of *doing* more, the key was *understanding* more? Creating real impact challenges us to question assumptions and recognise the interconnectedness of the systems we operate in. By embracing a broader perspective, we move beyond short-term fixes and create lasting solutions that benefit both individuals and the organisation as a whole.

The elephant parable is a reminder that acting on partial truths can lead us astray. Before we rush to new metrics, tighter deadlines, or another meeting, it helps to pause and ask, *"What am I not seeing? Whose voice is missing? What data have I ignored because it does not fit my first impression?"*

Empathy in Action: Transforming Teams

One manager we worked with at Dreem struggled to lead a team that was perpetually disengaged. Meetings were marked by silence, collaboration was rare, and deadlines often slipped. On the surface, the team didn't seem to care. The manager initially considered imposing stricter controls, but after some coaching and a few key questions, she paused.

She sat down with her team members one by one for honest, open conversations. She was surprised by what emerged. Her team members didn't feel seen or valued. Some felt that their ideas were dismissed too quickly, while others couldn't see how their work connected to the organisation's larger goals. What made the real difference, however, was her willingness to see feedback as a gift rather than a personal attack. Instead of taking the feedback personally, she listened to understand and stayed grounded in heart-centred leadership. This allowed her to remain calm, curious, and compassionate, qualities that kept her out of survival mode and opened the space for genuine transformation.

Armed with this understanding, she brought the team together. She acknowledged the communication gaps and worked with them to redefine their shared purpose. Slowly but surely, the team's energy shifted. Meetings became vibrant discussions. Collaboration increased exponentially. Within six months, the team was hitting every deadline and, more importantly, showing up with enthusiasm and ownership.

This change did not come from tighter controls but from empathy, connection, and the courage to lead from the heart. By addressing the root cause of disconnection and choosing understanding over reaction, she unlocked her team's collective potential within 6 months.

Coaching conversations that begin with empathy and curiosity become the bridge between awareness and meaningful change.

Mandela's Legacy: Leadership Rooted in Love

The implications of disconnection are reflected not only in organisations but also in wider societal dynamics. Fear drives division and pushes us toward control, micromanagement, and isolation, rather than meeting uncertainty with vulnerability and courage.

Nelson Mandela was imprisoned for twenty-seven years and spent long periods in solitude. It was during this time that he came to a profound realisation. He could not lead South Africa toward reconciliation while harbouring bitterness. To move the nation forward, he first had to let go of hatred.

Mandela's leadership was grounded in love and understanding, not as sentiment, but as discipline. By choosing dignity and respect in how he engaged with his former correctional officers, he dismantled fear-based barriers and transformed adversaries into allies. In doing so, he demonstrated that true leadership begins with inner reconciliation before it can create collective healing.

The day Nelson Mandela was released, his jailers reportedly wept. When asked by a journalist why they wept, they said they had lost their best friend. Mandela's profound empathy helped transform decades of oppression into an opportunity for healing, laying the groundwork for South Africa's path toward unity. As exemplified by Mandela's legacy, we have the opportunity to nurture growth and resilience, building a culture where everyone can thrive, even in the most unlikely circumstances

Creating an Enduring Legacy

It's not the title or the role that defines you. It's the legacy you leave behind. Whether we mean to or not, we all leave our mark.

So, ask yourself, *"What impact will I leave on the people, groups, and organisations I influence?" "Will people remember me as someone who made them feel seen and appreciated?" "Or will my legacy be one of disengagement, unresolved conflict, and fear-driven decisions, or have I inspired growth?"*

The most effective people recognise that their most significant influence comes from enabling others to develop and take charge of their own lives. A change in mindset is necessary, from dominance to cooperation and from rivalry to involvement. It's about creating an environment where others feel free to express themselves, grow, and succeed. Seeing oneself as part of something greater, a collective force for advancement and opportunity, not the focal point of the system, is what's needed for long-term influence. Aligning your beliefs with your vision, your decisions with your integrity, and your actions with the effect you want to have is ultimately what legacy is all about.

Ask yourself these questions;

- *What part of the "elephant" are you touching in your leadership or organisation? What might you discover if you opened yourself to seeing the whole?*
- *Where might fear be driving division in your team or organisation? How can you begin to address it?*
- *What might you learn if you made time for open, honest conversations?*
- *Where do silos exist in your organisation? How can you create opportunities for collaboration and shared purpose?*
- *What legacy would you like to leave behind?*

Prioritising Right Over Easy

Some view leadership as a pursuit of prestige, power, or caution. This way of thinking is common, yet it misses the deeper responsibility leadership carries. Leading from the heart asks for something more demanding and far more enduring.

Heart-centred leadership includes making difficult decisions, often when silence feels safer than speaking up. There are moments when giving up appears easier than standing your ground, and times when convenience tempts more than integrity. Leading from the heart does not remove these tensions. It asks us to meet them consciously. It shows up in the small, everyday decisions as much as in the defining moments.

People who lead from the heart do not default to the easiest path. Their judgments are not driven solely by self-interest or short-term gain. They are guided by values, even when that choice carries discomfort or cost. Influence, when disconnected from values, quickly becomes hollow. Its purpose is diminished when it serves only the self.

As I often remind myself:

"To live aligned with your values is to live fully. To deny them is to become a shell, trapped in a surface-level existence. The work, whether in coaching, business, or writing, comes from the same place: a commitment to truth, humanity, and freedom." - Reem Borrows

Not everyone needs to take severe measures or high-stake risks that could change their lives. However, operating from the heart shapes every decision, no matter how big or small it may seem.

The crucial questions to ask ourselves are:

- *How can I create a positive influence, however modest, without getting bogged down in the minutiae?*
- *Instead of ignoring unpleasant situations, how can I live courageously and lead in a way that is consistent with my values?*

It was while serving on a senior team in the corporate world that I came to understand the true weight of honesty. We were in one of our quarterly meetings, preparing to report back to our regional office, and the results were not positive. As a team, we had to face the uncomfortable reality that our numbers were poor.

Instead of addressing the situation openly, the unspoken rationale was to place two people leading one of the main teams on performance management. The blame for the wider team's poor results was now on them. After the meeting, I was pulled aside, and a story was shared with me about the global CEO addressing his global leadership team. This global CEO had announced that if his senior leadership team did not perform, he would replace them. If the next team failed, he would replace them again. And if the second team did not perform, then he would be replaced himself. The story was intended to highlight the harsh realities of accountability at the highest levels.

These decisions are made every day in many organisations. The closer look showed that the results reflected decisions made across the senior leadership team and were also shaped by external factors such as market fluctuations and government regulations. Honesty would have meant reporting that back clearly to our regional head office.

The message, however, reinforced a cycle of blame rather than a culture of learning. Some years later, after I had left the company, the entire senior leadership team had been replaced. Under new leadership, the culture shifted, and reporting became more transparent. The organisation began to thrive. Honesty proved to be not only a moral principle, but also a practical necessity. Without it, organisations risk solving the wrong problems. With it, they give themselves a chance to grow.

These five takeaways illustrate the role that courage and honesty play in creating trust, overcoming obstacles, and making a lasting impact.

1. **Adhere to Your Principles**

Your compass points to your values. Consider whether you are making decisions out of convenience or because you want to do what's right.

Captain Paul Watson, the founder of the Sea Shepherd Conservation Society and a co-founder of Greenpeace, is an example of someone who has remained loyal to their principles. When it came to defending marine life, Watson was uncompromising in his beliefs, even when it meant opposing governments, big businesses, and his own previous organisation. Paul was repeatedly detained, called an outlaw, and barred from several nations because of his aggressive non-violent interventions to defend marine life and ecosystems. However, he never wavered from his purpose.

The essence of the principle is not to do what is simple, but to do what is right.

2. **When It Counts, Speak Up**

Bravery doesn't remain silent in the face of injustice. Speaking out for something greater than yourself is what courageous leaders do.

Edward Snowden had a steady career and a bright future as a federal contractor. However, he risked everything to reveal the truth after learning of widespread monitoring programs that violated people's privacy. He lost his freedom, his house, and his citizenship, but he kept his moral character. He put principle ahead of his own safety.

Speaking out can be as simple as challenging prejudice in a meeting or standing up for a colleague who has experienced harassment or unfair treatment. At other times, it may involve questioning or reshaping practices that quietly allow injustice to persist. What matters is not the scale of the action, but the willingness to use our influence, in both small and significant ways, rather than staying silent because it feels easier or more comfortable.

3. **Become A Symbol of Something Greater Than Yourself.**

The 2025 ruling by U.S. District Judge Jesse Furman, an American Jew, who blocked the U.S. Immigration and Customs Enforcement (ICE) from deporting Mahmoud Khalil, a Palestinian academic with permanent United States residency, was an example of courage in action.

Furman could have opted for simplicity in response to demands from political organisations calling for his dismissal. He could have ignored the case, let the system decide, or avoided the criticism. Instead, he acted in alignment with justice and fairness, accepting that the consequences could include public backlash, institutional pressure, and personal cost.

4. **Put Character Before Comfort**

Standing up for your morals isn't always popular. You might encounter resistance, pass up opportunities, or have challenging conversations. When Facebook whistleblower Frances Haugen revealed how the corporation placed profit ahead of public safety, she lost her job, her reputation, and her security. But not her soul. Even when it meant facing one of the world's most influential companies, she chose truth over ease.

Those we admire are the ones who persevered through difficult times. Rather than using their position to further their interests, they chose to make the world more equitable. They didn't conveniently whitewash issues or avoid reality. They prioritised benefitting others before themselves. The world doesn't need any more people building wealth and prestige solely for themselves. It needs individuals prepared to lead with bravery, honesty, and compassion.

Questions to ponder:

- *How would you characterise honesty in leadership?*
- *What key ingredients do you need to develop further to succeed as a leader at this time and season?*

The Strength in Surrender

The Moment Everything Changed

The moment I let go was the moment that saved my life.

At 17, I went on a four-day bushwalk in the Northern Territory with a group of young people, camping under the stars and walking through rugged, red-earth country. On one of the last days, we stopped to rest at a waterfall. The air was still, and the view was beautiful from the top of the waterfall, where I sat with my dear friend Billy and a few others. Then, everything changed in an instant.

I slipped.

The water caught me and pulled me down the face of the waterfall so fast that there was no time to scream. No time to grab hold of anything. The current forced me into an underwater cave. I couldn't breathe. I couldn't see. I was completely submerged in pitch-black water, surrounded by four solid walls.

I didn't know which way was up. I started feeling around the cave, frantically searching for an exit. Every wall I touched was solid. No cracks. No light. Just water, pressure, fear, darkness, and the deafening silence of being completely alone. I kept searching, kept pushing, kept trying to fight my way out.

Nothing I tried was working.

Then something came over me. I stopped. I stopped fighting. I stopped panicking. I surrendered. I remember thinking, *"This is it. I'm going to die."* And in that moment, rather than resist, I let go.

That surrender is what saved me.

I blacked out. And while I was unconscious, my body, limp and unresisting, was carried by the current through a narrow opening. I floated out the other side and was pulled from the water by someone who saw me bobbing up and down.

I had no idea who I was or where I was. I had lost all my memory. In that haze, I saw Billy swim over to me. Although I didn't recognise her at that moment, I recognised something in her. I smiled. She calmed me and took me to dry land. After crossing to dry land, I still didn't know who I was, where I was, or what had just happened. The shock of it all overwhelmed me.

Later, Billy told me she had gone to find the opening I came out of. She said my body probably wouldn't have made it through the narrow space if I had been conscious and rigid. My body literally had to go with the flow. That's what saved me.

Bit by bit, my memory came back. The shock eventually passed. To this day, decades later, Billy still has that same calming effect on me. And the lesson never left.

I've reflected on that moment hundreds of times over the years. I've come to understand it wasn't just a physical experience. It was a spiritual one. A lesson in leadership, in life, and in the false belief that control keeps us safe.

Letting go didn't mean giving up. It meant releasing resistance. It meant trusting something bigger than myself. That single moment taught me something that may take a lifetime to integrate fully: **Real strength doesn't come from the grip. It comes from the release.**

We're taught to fight for everything. Push harder. Hold on tighter. Work more. Prove our worth.

But what if the tight grip is what's killing us?

Sometimes, the only way through is to stop fighting the current and let life carry us, in conscious trust. That's not a weakness. That's wisdom. The waterfall taught me that surrender is not about giving up. It's about accepting what is so that you can move with it, not against it. It's about recognising the moment you're in, taking a breath, and choosing presence over panic.

Surrender as a Leadership Practice

Surrender isn't a one-time event. It's a practice. A mindset. A way of being. It doesn't mean you don't plan, lead, or take action. But it does mean you don't grip so hard that you lose the ability to see what life, or your team, is showing you.

Some of the most significant breakthroughs don't come from trying harder. They come from stillness, trusting the process, releasing the need to prove anything. From trusting that what you have built within yourself will carry you through.

If you're in a moment right now where things feel stuck, heavy, or hard...ask yourself:

- *What am I resisting?*
- *Where am I gripping?*
- *What would happen if I softened, just a little?*
- *What if letting go is the very thing that opens the door?*

Section Three

Gratitude and Relationship Intelligence

Chapter 7

Gratitude

Embracing Failure and Conflict
as Growth Opportunities

"Gratitude helps you to grow and expand; gratitude brings joy and laughter into your life and into the lives of all those around you."[1]
— Eileen Caddy

Why Gratitude Matters: The Individual Perspective

Gratitude isn't just about recognising what's going well. It's about choosing how we respond to life's ups and downs. Gratitude offers us a choice. In any situation, we can choose to focus on what's wrong and stay stuck in the problem, or we can acknowledge what's working, what's still possible, and what's worth appreciating.

Given that our brains are wired to zero in on problems, replay them, and stay stuck in them, we often believe that focusing on the issue means we are somehow solving it.[2] This mindset can trap us. Problems beget problems. Negativity breeds more negativity. Gratitude, on the other hand, interrupts this cycle. It shifts our focus toward solutions, possibilities, and progress. It's not about ignoring problems. It's about recognising them, then choosing to focus on what's good and what can be done. What you focus on expands. If you focus on solutions, they start to appear. Gratitude gives you the clarity and resilience to navigate challenges with a growth mindset. And this mindset isn't only good for you; it's contagious. The way you approach life has a ripple effect on those around you.

From Problems to Possibilities

Focusing on gratitude sounds simple, yet changing human behaviour rarely is. Having worked with teams across many industries and levels, I have seen the same challenges repeat themselves in organisation after organisation. People love focusing on problems. One could argue that people, unknowingly, are addicted to problems and only feel useful if they focus on issues and create more work for themselves. Most of us live in a perpetual state of victimhood without even realising it. You may think that observation sounds harsh, but if you're paying attention, you'll quickly observe how much complaining is going on and how unhappy people sound.

Gratitude brings us back to what truly matters. Success grows through strategy and effort, and it is sustained through the relationships we choose to nurture.

When I first started my career, my manager shared with me, "True leadership is when you can influence people's behaviour for the better and let them feel like it was their idea." It's about the people you mentor, support, and encourage along the way. The trust, bonds, and relationships we share with those we lead put our priorities into perspective. When you express gratitude, you strengthen connections, you build trust, and you transform workplaces into spaces where everyone feels valued and empowered to thrive.

Gratitude: The Silent Strength

Gratitude goes deeper than a simple "thank you" or a polite formality. It can shift perspectives, heal wounds, and create stronger relationships. When you genuinely appreciate someone's efforts, you acknowledge their task and contribution, sending a stronger message: *You matter. What you bring to the table is recognised, valued, and vital.* People want to feel significant. They want to feel like they add value and that what they do makes a difference.

When you express appreciation, you encourage others to see the possibilities, shifting the mindset from fixating on problems to seeking solutions.

The Ripple Effect of Gratitude

When gratitude is part of daily interactions, meetings become spaces where small wins are celebrated alongside big achievements. Team members begin to work together and support one another, knowing their contributions are recognised and appreciated. In such an environment, morale rises, collaboration strengthens, and productivity flourishes because people feel seen and valued.

When you focus on gratitude, you create a culture where wins multiply. This shift changes everything.

Gratitude in Action: Practical Steps

At Dreem, we help teams build gratitude into their daily rhythm. Gratitude is the antidote to chaos. It grounds people in appreciation and perspective.

Start the Day with Intention:
A few words of appreciation can transform the tone of a meeting or an entire day. Try opening a team huddle with something simple: "I'm grateful for the energy you're bringing today. We've got some exciting challenges ahead, and I couldn't ask for a better team." Starting from gratitude shifts focus from problems to possibilities.

The Unexpected Thank-You:

Early in my career, a senior leader stopped by my desk and said, "I've noticed how organised your workspace always is. It says a lot about how you think. Keep it up, your results show it." It was a small gesture, but it made a lasting impression. I hadn't realised he had even noticed me. That one sentence fuelled my confidence.

Make Feedback Meaningful:

A simple thank-you is good, but meaningful gratitude recognises the unseen effort behind the results. For example: "I know you stayed late to get this presentation right. The clarity you brought to those ideas made a real difference. Thank you." This type of feedback builds connection, loyalty, and intrinsic motivation far more effectively than performance reviews alone.

Create Shared Gratitude Moments:

I've known people to hold on to notes from their team members for years and years. Only recently, an old schoolmate reached out to tell me he had kept a note I wrote to him back in 1986, and that it still put a smile on his face. I had completely forgotten about it and still can't remember writing it, yet it's a reminder of how often we don't realise the impact we have on others. You may not be able to change the world, but you can change someone's world.

Make Gratitude a Habit:

Dedicate time each week to celebrate small wins. Even a simple Friday reflection, highlighting one or two contributions, can reinforce the value of progress over perfection. Gratitude, practised consistently, positively impacts culture. It reminds us that leadership is about connection. When you focus on what is going right, even during difficult moments, a mindset of appreciation becomes the foundation for dealing with setbacks and conflict with calm, clarity, and perspective.

The 4-Step Process for Turning Setbacks into Solutions: From Gratitude to Growth

I've been fortunate enough to be surrounded by Bob Procter and other great coaches and mentors who challenge me and move me beyond my comfort zone.

Throughout my years in the corporate space, I was trained in many areas of organisational psychology. I was accredited to deliver programs that taught me practical application, a focus that continues to this day. I took part in the NAU ASIAPAC LEADERSHIP PEAK Programs, the flagship of the Accelerated Leadership Development programs for Novartis Asia/Harvard University in Shanghai and also became a graduate of the Australian Institute of Company Directors. I would travel to Canada every six months to work with Bob, and each time I visited, I wanted to showcase what I had created, from PowerPoint presentations to leadership and strategy frameworks.

During one memorable visit, I shared a conflict-resolution framework I had recently developed and delivered to a team with strong results. I explained that while gratitude is essential, people also need support to navigate conflict, especially when gratitude practices are resisted amid unresolved tension. I walked him through the framework. He listened, appreciated the thinking behind it, and then paused before asking a simple question: "Reem, why do organisations like to complicate everything?"

I asked if he was referring to the framework just presented, and he was.

"Simplicity is key to changing human behaviour, Reem," he responded. Bob then shared a simple three-step process, drawn from his friend Michael Bernard Beckwith's work, to help individuals navigate failure and conflict. He encouraged me to translate it into a framework that organisations could use and to test it in real settings.

I did exactly that, adding one additional step along the way. The process has since been tested across several organisations, and its strength lies in its simplicity. People remember it easily and apply it quickly. While I still draw on the depth of knowledge and expertise gained through my formal studies, the model itself remains straightforward and accessible.

Here's the 4-step technique that came from that process:

Step 1: It is what it is, accept it

Acceptance is the first stage in dealing with disagreement or failure. This entails accepting that, whether you like it or not, the circumstances have developed as they have.

Acceptance is acknowledging what happened without becoming stuck in annoyance or, worse, denial. Accepting *what is* acknowledges what happened and does not necessarily need approval.

Scenario:

I was working with an organisation on its operating rhythm and on embedding the GROW model coaching approach with its leaders when I was asked to mediate a situation between two senior leaders. They had once worked closely and effectively together until a single incident created a rupture neither could move past. By the time we sat down together, they could barely look at one another, and the impact on the wider team was unmistakable.

We sat around a table in a small meeting room. I stood by the flip chart.

I said, "Before we go anywhere else, I want to start with this."

I wrote at the top of the page: *What happened?*

I turned back to them. "I'd like each of you to share what you experienced."

One spoke first, then the other. The details differed, but the emotion underneath was clear. Frustration. Disappointment. Hurt. As they spoke, neither interrupted.

When they finished, I asked, "Is there anything either of you can do to change what has already happened?"

There was a pause.

One of them shook his head. "No."

The other added, "Nothing on this earth can reverse time."

I nodded and let that sit for a moment.

"Alright," I replied. "If we agree that what happened cannot be undone, can I move us to the next step? It's a harder one."

They both hesitated, then agreed.

I turned back to the flip chart and wrote the next line.

Step 2: Harvest the Good

Every failure and conflict, no matter how painful, has something valuable to teach you. *Harvesting the good* means identifying the situation's positives, lessons, and opportunities for growth.

This mindset allows you to reframe the experience and turn it into a productive learning moment.

Scenario:

I turned back to the flip chart and wrote the next question.

"Is there anything either of you learnt from this experience?"

There was a longer pause this time.

One of them spoke first. "Yes. More than I expected."

The other nodded. "Same."

"OK, let's write it down." I encouraged them to take a few moments.

As they spoke, I captured their words on the flip chart. They talked about how quickly trust can fracture, how fragile human behaviour can be under pressure, and how easily assumptions take hold. At one point, one of them said, quietly, "We both let our egos get in the way."

The other looked at the list and said, "I can see that now too."

By the time we finished, there were five or six points written clearly on the page. I stepped back and let them read what they had just named for themselves.

After a moment, I asked, "Are you willing to move to the next step?"

They both agreed.

Step 3: Forgive the Rest

I wrote the final heading on the flip chart: **Forgive the rest.**

I explained gently, "Forgiveness here is not about justifying what happened or deciding who was right or wrong. It's about letting go of what is still weighing you down so you can move forward."

They listened closely.

"For some people," I continued, "the harder part is forgiving the other person. For others, it's forgiving themselves. Either way, forgiveness is not really about the other person at all. It's about releasing the emotional weight that keeps you stuck."

One of them exhaled slowly. The other nodded.

"It's about freeing yourselves," I added, "so this no longer defines how you work, how you lead, or how you relate to one another."

The room was quiet, but the shift was unmistakable.

Forgiveness, at its core, is the decision to release what no longer serves you. It is the act of letting go of emotional weight, not to excuse what happened, but to prevent it from shaping what comes next. Whether forgiveness is directed outward or inward, its purpose is the same. It restores movement. It allows clarity to return. And it creates space to move forward without carrying the past into every future interaction.

Scenario:

I could feel the hesitation in the room. Both wanted a resolution, but neither was eager to go any further.

I shared, "This part isn't easy. And we don't need to force it."

They both looked relieved by that.

"So let's slow it down," I continued. "Before we go any further, I want to ask you something simpler."

I picked up the marker again. "What do you actually want from here?"

They spoke carefully at first. One said he wanted peace at work. The other said he wanted to stop carrying the tension into every meeting. I wrote their words on the flip chart as they spoke.

We talked through what moving forward might look like in practice, not in theory. What they wanted to let go of. What they were tired of holding onto.

Then I asked, "Let me ask you one more thing. In this situation, is it more important to be right or to be kind?"

Neither answered straight away.

One of them eventually said, "Being right hasn't helped much so far."

The other nodded. "No. It hasn't."

Something shifted then. Shoulders dropped. The tone softened. You could see the weight lift as they let go of what they had been carrying for far too long.

After a moment, I asked, "Are you ready to move to the next step?"

This time, they didn't hesitate.

Step 4: Determine the Next Step

Only after completing the first three steps with honesty and authenticity do you move to this stage. It's a bit like the game of Monopoly. You can't collect the $200 until you pass Go.

At this point, it's time to act. You have acknowledged the circumstances, reflected on what occurred, and released what needed to be forgiven. From here, the focus shifts forward.

Determine the next course of action by identifying what needs to change to resolve the issue or prevent it from happening again. The aim is to create a clear, practical strategy that restores direction and supports better outcomes moving ahead.

Scenario:

We looked back at the flip chart together and shifted the conversation to what would change from here.

One of them spoke first. "Moving forward, budgets should be set together."

The other nodded. "And presented to the CEO jointly."

There was a pause, then the second added, "We also need to be more aligned on supply chain questions coming from overseas. No more working it out separately."

Both agreed to that immediately. It was practical, specific, and shared.

Before we wrapped up, I checked in once more. "Are you both comfortable with what you've agreed to here?"

"Yes," one said.

"Yes," the other followed.

The shift in the room was unmistakable.

I was later told they went to lunch together the very next day, after a long period of not being able to sit at the same table.

Moments like this remind us that conflict and failure are unavoidable. What determines growth is how we meet them. Missed opportunities, strained relationships, and business setbacks can either harden positions or refine them.

That is why this process belongs in the gratitude chapter. The very situations that test us are often the ones that sharpen our thinking, strengthen our relationships, and expand our leadership capacity. Without them, growth remains abstract. With them, it becomes real.

How to View Failure and Conflict?

Many of us are conditioned to measure success, and even our sense of worth, by outcomes. When results fall short or conflict arises, that attachment can quietly turn into pressure, disappointment, and self-doubt.

When attention stays fixed on the end result, people often lose interest in the process itself. The journey becomes secondary to the destination, and stress replaces learning. This mindset distorts how we define success and limits our capacity to grow.

Think about medical research. Scientists working to cure a disease do not judge success by whether the cure appears immediately. Progress comes through testing, observation, and it's a process of elimination. Each failed trial is not treated as a mistake, but as valuable information. What does not work narrows the path toward what eventually will.

In this way, failure becomes part of the process rather than evidence of inadequacy. Progress is measured by learning, refinement, and persistence, not by instant results.

The same applies to personal development and leadership. When we focus on the process rather than the outcome, we build resilience. Setbacks and conflict become teachers rather than threats. Without them, learning stalls. Growth depends on staying engaged with the work itself, trusting that clarity and capability emerge through consistent effort over time.

Reflection: Gratitude in Action: Practical Steps

Let's explore ways to incorporate gratitude into the workplace.

Gratitude strengthens focus, resilience, and connection when it becomes part of the daily rhythm rather than an occasional gesture. The following practical steps can be used by individuals and teams to embed gratitude into everyday work life.

1. Start the Day with Gratitude

Take five minutes at the start of each day to note three things you are grateful for. These can be as simple as a productive conversation, a colleague's support, or an opportunity to contribute. Encourage teams to share one highlight during weekly meetings to reinforce positive momentum.

2. Reframe Setbacks

When something doesn't go to plan, pause before reacting. Identify one thing that still went well, and one lesson the situation revealed. Use this as a learning moment in team debriefs to shift focus from blame to growth.

3. Acknowledge Others Regularly

Look for opportunities to express genuine appreciation in the moment. A brief "thank you" for someone's effort, reliability, or attitude goes a long way. You can set the tone by modelling frequent, specific recognition.

4. Create a Culture of Appreciation

Establish small rituals such as a "gratitude round" at the start of meetings, or a shared gratitude board where team members can post acknowledgments. Consistency helps gratitude evolve from an act to a habit.

5. Use Gratitude to Build Resilience

- Encourage individuals and teams to close each week by asking:
- What worked well? What did we learn? What do we appreciate about each other?
- This reflection keeps the focus on progress, strengthens team connection, and reinforces confidence through change or challenge.

Chapter 8

Knowing Yourself and Understanding Others

"Until you make the unconscious conscious, it will direct your life, and you will call it fate."[1]
— Carl Jung

Throughout this book, we have explored the unseen forces that shape our lives. Like the iceberg model we discussed earlier, much of what drives human behaviour remains hidden beneath the surface.

In this chapter, our focus now shifts to the visible world of behaviour and communication, where our preferences, choices, and actions come to life. These visible expressions are shaped by what lies underneath, yet they are also how we influence and connect with those around us.

To understand the bridge between the inner and outer worlds, we turn to the pioneering work of Carl Jung, the Swiss psychiatrist and psychoanalyst whose theories have reshaped modern psychology. Jung taught that self-awareness develops through recognising and integrating all parts of ourselves.

Every pattern we display in thought, emotion, or behaviour has roots in both the conscious and the unconscious.[2] Understanding these behavioural preferences also reveals that not everyone communicates, thinks, or works in the same way. Each person has a natural style and preference in any given situation, and when we understand both our own and others' preferences, we can adapt. This adaptability is at the heart of emotionally intelligent leadership. It helps us communicate more effectively, manage conflict with empathy, and create stronger, more balanced teams.

In this chapter, we will explore the connection between self-awareness, perception, emotional intelligence, and decision-making, before introducing the **Insights Discovery** framework. This model, inspired by Jung's work, helps us recognise different behavioural styles, understand our natural tendencies, and adapt them to build trust, collaboration, and influence.

Insights Discovery is one of several well-established frameworks we work with in this space.[3] Depending on context and need, we also draw on tools such as DiSC, HBDI, StrengthsFinder, MBTI, and others. The principles explored in this chapter apply across these models, with the framework serving as a lens rather than a limitation.

The Ladder of Perception: How Assumptions Shape Reality

The Ladder of Perception

Actions I took

Beliefs I formed

Emotional and physical responses

Logical conclusions I drew

Interpretations and meanings I gave

Value judgements I made

My perception (selected data)

The event (as a camera would capture it)

The Perception Ladder. Source: The Insights Group LTD, 2014-2019.

The Ladder of Perception is a model that explains how we process external stimuli and form conclusions. The steps include:

- **Observation**: We take in raw data from our surroundings.
- **Selection**: We filter the information we focus on based on past experiences, personal biases, and what feels most relevant at the moment. What we miss is that the selected data is not all the available data. It is only what our minds have chosen to notice.
- **Value Judgement**: We make a value judgement on that interpreted data, deciding whether it is right or wrong, good or bad, based on our experiences, core values, and beliefs.
- **Interpretation**: We assign meaning to the selected information.

- **Assumption**: We develop assumptions shaped by our interpretations, value judgements and beliefs.
- **Conclusion**: We draw conclusions and reinforce our existing beliefs.
- **Action**: We react based on those conclusions.

This process happens instantly and often unconsciously, meaning much of what we believe about a situation is shaped by our existing worldview rather than objective reality. Once we form a belief at the top of the ladder, confirmation bias kicks in. We start looking for more examples to prove ourselves right, further strengthening that belief, whether or not it is accurate. The challenge is learning to slow down, question our process, and recognise when our perception may be incomplete or biased.

For example:

- We have seen how quickly stories form in the absence of information. Someone sends an email and hears nothing back for days. The silence can feel personal. Assumptions creep in about being dismissed or deliberately ignored. When people eventually speak, the reality is far less dramatic. The recipient had been buried in back-to-back meetings, had read the message, and genuinely believed they had already replied.
- What about when capable team members sit quietly through meetings and are written off as being disengaged? We come to our own conclusions only to realise, in a one-on-one conversation, that the same person had articulated the issue with clarity and depth, having spent time listening, processing, and thinking before speaking.

Recognising the impact of perception and assumptions allows us to challenge our knee-jerk reactions, come back down the ladder, ask better questions, and engage with others more thoughtfully.

Self-Regulation in Decision-Making

Decision-making is often described as a logical, data-driven process. In reality, every decision is shaped by emotional, psychological, and unconscious influences that operate beneath the surface. What matters most is not the absence of emotion, but our capacity to recognise what is at play within us and to prevent it from quietly driving our choices.

From a psychological perspective, self-regulation begins with self-awareness. This involves more than noticing how you feel in the moment. It requires understanding where those feelings come from and how they influence behaviour. When people are unaware of why certain situations trigger discomfort, urgency, or overcompensation, their decisions are shaped by emotion rather than guided by intention. These patterns are often rooted in unresolved experiences or inherited emotional scripts that continue to operate unless they are brought into awareness.

For example, a leader who constantly seeks approval may avoid necessary confrontation without realising why. What feels like empathy on the surface may in fact be driven by an unexamined fear of rejection. Another leader may take on the role of rescuer or martyr, making decisions that appear selfless but are guided by a deep psychological pattern rather than by what best serves the team or organisation.

Self-regulation interrupts this emotional scripting. When a strong emotion such as fear, anger, or shame arises, self-regulation allows us to pause and choose not to let that emotion determine what happens next. This is not about suppressing or denying feelings. It is about becoming curious about what is driving them. Asking simple but honest questions such as *"Why am I reacting this way? What story or perceived threat is being activated?* "creates space between stimulus and response. That pause is a marker of emotional maturity.

As self-regulation strengthens, empathy naturally follows. Empathy allows us to recognise that resistance, disengagement, or hostility in others often reflects unspoken fears, frustrations, or competing loyalties rather than defiance or lack of commitment. Leaders who develop this awareness are less likely to personalise behaviour and more capable of responding with clarity and steadiness.

Self-regulation in decision-making supports clear, courageous judgment while honouring the complexity of human emotion. Before reaching a conclusion, it helps to pause and ask:

- *How will this decision affect those around me?*
- *Am I reacting from emotion, or responding with perspective?*
- *What assumptions or unconscious biases might be influencing my thinking?*

Holding these questions in mind allows decisions to be made with greater balance and discernment. Over time, this practice strengthens leadership effectiveness, trust, and the quality of outcomes, not because emotion is removed, but because it is understood and integrated.

Understanding Behavioural Preferences Through Insights Discovery

At DREEM, we work with a range of accredited behavioural and leadership frameworks, selecting the most appropriate tool for the context and the people involved. One of these is the Insights Discovery model, which draws on Jung's theory of personality preferences. We often use Insights because it offers a practical, accessible way to understand behaviour, relationships, and communication, and it translates easily into everyday leadership practice.

My business partner and dear friend, Gloria Rees, and I are both accredited in Insights Discovery; Gloria also serves on the Global Faculty and is an Insights Partner. When we use this framework, it is as a lens rather than a label, helping individuals and organisations explore the deeper drivers behind behaviour and adapt how they engage with others to improve communication, trust, and effectiveness.

We have seen the impact of this framework time and again. Leaders who once struggled to engage their teams become more empathetic and influential. Teams that once operated in silos transform into collaborative, trusting, and high-performing groups. Businesses shift from experiencing communication breakdowns and misunderstandings to building cultures of openness, respect, and appreciation for diversity. Insights Discovery gives people a shared language for understanding human differences, and that shared language becomes the foundation for lasting change.

Instead of labelling individuals, Insights Discovery identifies situational, fluid behavioural preferences. This focus helps individuals adapt their approach to varying circumstances.[3]

At its core, Insights Discovery is built on three key principles:

1. **Individuality:** Each person has unique preferences and strengths, shaping how they interact with the world.
2. **Positive Focus:** The model encourages self-reflection and growth by emphasising strengths rather than limiting individuals to fixed categories.
3. **Psychological Foundation:** Insights Discovery offers a structured lens on human behaviour and communication.

Rather than assigning rigid personality types, Insights Discovery describes four sets of behavioural preferences, represented by four colour energies:

- **Fiery Red:** Action-oriented, decisive, and results-driven. When people use Fiery Red energy, they prefer directness, efficiency, and quick decision-making.
- **Sunshine Yellow:** Enthusiastic, people-focused, and adaptable. Sunshine Yellow energy is associated with creativity, sociability, and the ability to inspire others.
- **Earth Green:** Supportive, values-driven, and steady. People with strong Earth Green energy prioritise relationships, harmony, and deep connections.
- **Cool Blue:** Analytical, precise, and detail-oriented. Those who lean towards Cool Blue energy value accuracy, structure, and logical thinking.

Most people exhibit a blend of these behavioural preferences, shifting between them according to situational needs. Self-awareness begins with understanding which preferences we naturally lean toward, how they influence our interactions, and how others may perceive these behaviours.

Adapting Our behaviour to Different behavioural Preferences

We all have the ability to flex our communication style to connect better with others once we understand our preferences and theirs. Here are some ways to recognise and adapt to different behavioural preferences:

- When communicating with someone who prefers Fiery Red energy, be direct, concise, and focused on results. Avoid over-explaining or being vague.

- When engaging with someone who prefers Sunshine Yellow energy, be enthusiastic, open, and engaging. Show appreciation for their ideas and creativity.
- When working with someone who prefers Earth Green energy, show empathy, be patient, and create a collaborative environment. Avoid being too forceful or abrupt.
- When interacting with someone displaying a preference for Cool Blue energy, be logical, provide data, and allow time for reflection. Avoid pressuring them into quick decisions.

Perceived Good Day and Bad Day behaviour: A Matter of Perspective

Because our own behavioural preferences shape our perceptions, what we perceive as someone's "bad day" behaviour may not necessarily indicate that they are having a bad day at all. What feels natural to one person might be seen as challenging or off-putting to another, simply because of differences in communication and preferred working styles. Being mindful of our perceptions helps us move away from judgment and toward understanding.

The four behavioural preferences, Fiery Red, Sunshine Yellow, Earth Green, and Cool Blue, have strengths that shine on a "good day" and behaviours that might be misinterpreted on a "bad day." The key is recognising that these behaviours may be perceived differently by others with contrasting preferences.

Fiery Red Energy

- Good Day Perception: Confident, decisive, focused, results-driven, action-oriented, efficient.

- Perceived Bad Day behaviour: Aggressive, impatient, overly direct, dismissive, controlling.

A person using fiery red energy prefers speed, clarity, and results. This energy can come across as too forceful or lacking consideration to someone with a more reflective or relational approach (like Earth Green). The key to working with Fiery Red energy is not taking directness personally and understanding the intention is often to drive progress, not offend.

Sunshine Yellow Energy

- Good Day Perception: Enthusiastic, charismatic, engaging, energetic, inspirational.
- Perceived Bad Day behaviour: overly talkative, scattered, attention-seeking, easily distracted, unfocused.

Sunshine Yellow thrives on connection and spontaneity. This energy might feel chaotic or lacking discipline to someone with a more structured, detail-focused approach (like Cool Blue). Sunshine Yellow energy is a catalyst for creativity and engagement. The key is to balance enthusiasm with focus.

Earth Green Energy

- Good Day Perception: Supportive, patient, loyal, empathetic, values-driven, harmonious.
- Perceived Bad Day behaviour: Passive, resistant to change, overly sensitive, indecisive, avoidant of confrontation.

Earth Green energy prioritises harmony and deep relationships. To someone with a fast-paced, results-driven approach (Fiery Red preference), this energy may be perceived as too slow or lacking urgency. However, in environments that require team cohesion and trust, Earth Green Energy is a stabilising force. The key to working with Earth Green is understanding the need for alignment and reassurance.

Cool Blue Energy

- Good Day Perception: Analytical, precise, logical, objective, structured, detail-oriented.
- Perceived Bad Day behaviour: Cold, detached, overly critical, inflexible, slow to act.

Cool Blue energy values structure, logic, and accuracy. This energy might feel overly rigid or distant to someone with a more free-flowing, people-focused approach (Sunshine Yellow preference). However, when it comes to data-driven decision-making and long-term strategy, Cool Blue Energy provides depth and clarity. The key is to give Cool Blue preference time to process information and to respect the need for thoroughness.

> *"Everything that irritates us about others can lead us to an understanding of ourselves,"*
> - Carl Jung

Behavioural Preferences Are Not an Excuse for "Bad Day" behaviour.

While understanding our behavioural preferences is essential, never use them as an excuse for poor behaviour. Just because someone has a strong Fiery Red preference does not mean they have free rein to be blunt or dismissive, nor does a Cool Blue preference justify disengagement or overanalysing to the point of inaction.

The key to personal and professional growth is recognising our triggers when stress, fatigue, or unchecked ego lead us into counterproductive or even harmful patterns, and then approaching them with emotional intelligence.

A valuable exercise for effectively navigating your own behaviour patterns is to pause the moment you identify a feeling or trigger and ask:

- *What is really happening beneath the surface? Am I reacting from a place of stress, fear, or insecurity?*
- *How is my behaviour impacting those around me? Am I unintentionally pushing others away or creating tension?*
- *Am I missing something? Is there another way I could look at this situation?*
- *Have I run up my ladder, or do I need to come back down?*
- *What would a more mindful response look like? How can I adjust my approach to align with my values and build or maintain trust?*

Regularly reflecting on these questions can ensure that our behavioural preferences enhance our interactions rather than hinder them. Self-awareness involves understanding how we prefer to operate and manage our behaviours.

Additional Resource: Insights Discovery

As a companion to this chapter, you can download the full Insights Discovery e-book written by Gloria Rees, a specialist in this field, by visiting dreem.com.au/lead-differently to access the download. This resource is packed with valuable tools and perspectives and will serve as a treasure for anyone looking to deepen their understanding.

The e-book is complimentary as part of your purchase of Unfollow the Leader. If you would like to go further and have an individual or team report generated, you can contact us at info@dreem.com.au

Week-long Reflective Exercise

This activity is designed to enhance your self-regulation by helping you understand the underlying emotions behind your actions and adapt your leadership style to others' behavioural preferences.

Emotional Intelligence and Behavioural Awareness: A Five-Step Reflection

1. **Reflect on a key decision.**
   - Think of a recent decision that carried emotional weight. Note what you chose, who was involved, and how you felt before, during, and after.
2. **Recognise emotional patterns.**
   - Identify the emotions you experienced and trace their roots. Ask:
     - Is this feeling tied to past experiences or beliefs?
     - Could it reflect a broader human pattern, such as fear, control, or belonging?
3. **Understand emotional influence**
   - Ask how your emotions shaped your response.
   - Were you guided by values or avoiding discomfort?
   - Did fear, pride, or approval-seeking influence your action?
4. **Practise emotional agility**.
   - Create space between emotion and action. Use short pauses, self-talk, or reflection to choose deliberate responses.
5. **5. Adapt and connect**
   - Observe others' communication styles: flex your approach to meet them where they are. End each week by asking:
     - What patterns drive my decisions?

- How has adapting improved connection and outcomes?
- What will I do differently next time?

- How has adapting improved connection and outcomes?
- What will I do differently next time?

Section Four

Strategy in Motion

Practical Steps for Leadership Execution

Chapter 9

Leading with Flow

Aligning Purpose, Values, and Impact

"Whatever you do in your business comes out of a state of inner alignment with life and the source of life itself, so peace flows into whatever you do."[1]
— Eckhart Tolle

You know those moments when everything clicks? When work doesn't feel like a struggle, and things seem to flow? The way we show up in business and in life is a direct reflection of our inner alignment. But how often do we really feel that kind of flow?

The Flow State: The Highest Form of Human Experience

When you're in the zone, when time seems to fall away and what you're doing feels meaningful, you're in flow.[2] It's the pinnacle of human experience, the point at which your strengths are put to the test, and you perform at your peak. Flow is not about working harder or pushing through. It emerges when the right conditions are in place.

Creating flow is about building environments where people can flourish, not just improving efficiency. Flow grows from clarity, autonomy, and meaningful work. What matters most is creating the conditions that allow people to find purpose and satisfaction in what they do. When flow becomes part of a team's culture, people don't just do more, they contribute with energy, creativity, and a sense of alignment.

Success need not be a struggle. We are often told that achieving meaningful goals requires constant effort, sacrifice, and grind. Yet there is another way. One that sustains rather than exhausts. One that fuels engagement rather than draining it.

Think of a river. Water does not fight what stands in its way. It does not waste energy resisting rocks or obstacles. It moves around them, over them, or beneath them, continuing forward without force. It adapts and keeps moving. This is how individuals, teams, and organisations can operate. Flow emerges naturally when there is clarity about direction, a structure that supports progress, and the discipline to focus on what adds value while letting go of what does not.

Flow is not something you force. It is something you allow by setting a strong foundation. It comes from presence, from letting go of attachment to outcomes, and from giving full attention to one task at a time.

The Power of Presence in Flow

The key to flow is being fully present in every task. As mentioned earlier, when we focus too much on an outcome, whether it's winning a deal, completing a project, or hitting a target, we instantly block creativity and momentum.

Take sales, for example. A great salesperson does not fixate on whether the customer says yes or no. That final decision always belongs to the customer. What *is* within the salesperson's responsibility is the process that leads there. Understanding the customer's needs, listening deeply, adding genuine value, closing gaps through relevant solutions, and addressing objections with clarity and respect.

When a salesperson focuses on these fundamentals and does them well, closing becomes a natural outcome rather than a forced moment. The role of the salesperson is to create clarity and confidence. The customer's role is to choose. When each person owns their part, the conversation stays grounded, authentic, and effective.

The best lesson I was taught decades ago is that I *begin* to make a sale when I receive a <u>no</u>. My role was to:

- Be clear on what the customer wants
- Build the correct structure (territory/call plan)
- Show up consistently
- Ask the right questions to understand the customers' needs
- Maintain the right mindset and be fully present

When salespeople do these things without attachment to the outcome, they build authentic relationships and long-term success. This principle of presence applies to everything: leadership, business, and life. The outcome is not always in your control, but the process is. Set the proper foundation, stay present, and let the results unfold naturally.

The 5 Steps to Flow – The Path of Least Resistance

You can do things the easy way or the hard way. The choice is always yours. Hard work can lead to success, but it often comes at a cost: exhaustion, imbalance, or disconnection from what truly matters. Flow offers another path, the path of least resistance, where effort still exists but feels lighter, aligned, and sustainable.

The process is always the same. Here are the five steps we build to create flow for individuals, teams, and organisations at large.

A Note Before the Five Steps

You may notice that the ideas in the next section feel familiar. That is intentional. Insight alone rarely creates change. Real growth happens through repetition, practice, and application over time.

Earlier in the book, these principles were explored as concepts. Here, they are brought together into a five-step process so they can be lived, not just understood. This is not repetition for the sake of emphasis. It is integration.

When ideas are revisited in a new structure, they land differently. What once felt abstract becomes practical. What was once intuitive becomes deliberate. This is how awareness turns into action, and action into consistent behaviour.

Think of these steps as anchors you can return to. You won't always need all five at once. At different moments, one step will matter more than the others. The power comes from knowing they are available, connected, and designed to work together.

Read them slowly. Let them settle. These are not steps to rush through, but practices to return to as life and leadership continue to test you.

1. Clarity: Know What You Want

If you don't know precisely what you want, you'll waste time reacting to circumstances instead of shaping them. You would never get into a car and ask Siri or the navigator to take you *somewhere*; you ask for a specific location. In leadership, clarity means defining a vision for yourself and your team.

- In sales, clarity means understanding your role to serve, educate, and build trust, rather than chasing the results.
- In life, clarity means knowing what truly matters to you and avoiding distractions that don't align with it.

Ask yourself, *what do I really want? What truly aligns with who I am?*

If you lead an organisation, what is your purpose and ultimate goal? Then, break it down into aligned actions for teams and individuals.

2. Structure: Build the Reporting Lines and the Right Operating Rhythm that is Going to Support Your Goal

Without structure, water would run everywhere, never gaining momentum. The same applies to leadership, business, and personal success. In leadership, finding the rhythm means setting up systems for decision-making, meetings, engagement, and accountability.

- In sales, it's about a territory and a call plan for consistency, knowing who to call, when to call, and how often.
- In life, it's about creating daily habits that keep you focused and energised.

Ask yourself, *"What daily or weekly structures will effortlessly support my goals?"*

For an organisation, ask, *"What operating rhythm do we need to support our goals moving forward?"*

If we do not consciously choose the right operating rhythm that aligns with our goals and purpose, we end up in chaos.

3. Emotional Management: Create Order

Flow requires us to manage emotions rather than getting stuck in them. Emotional management and consistency support clearly defined goals and keep our efforts flowing in the direction we choose.

The ability to learn from our mistakes and see them as blessings empowers us to take the next step, and then the next. How else could we grow?

- In leadership, emotional management means handling conflict calmly and making clear-headed decisions.
- In sales, it's about not taking rejection or setbacks personally. A *no* is not about you. It's about the customer's needs and timing.
- In life, it means embracing uncertainty instead of fearing it.

Ask yourself, *"How do I react when things don't go my way? Do I flow around obstacles, or do I fight them?"*

In an organisation, ask whether you have built a culture of coaching for transformation and support, where constructive conflict is welcomed, and mistakes are seen as opportunities to learn.

4. Appreciation & Gratitude: Focus on What's Working

What you focus on expands. When you celebrate small wins and acknowledge progress, momentum builds naturally.

A common mistake is constantly chasing the next target without appreciating what's already working. But a culture of appreciation fuels confidence, motivation, and long-term success. What you focus on expands. When you celebrate small wins and acknowledge progress, momentum builds naturally.

- In leadership, recognise and celebrate team wins: big or small.
- In sales, focus on building relationships over time instead of obsessing over a single transaction.
- In life, acknowledge progress instead of fixating on what's missing.

Ask yourself, *"What's already working that I can appreciate today?"*

5. Flow State: Let It Happen

Once the first four steps are in place, flow happens naturally. You can't force it. Flow happens when you create the right conditions.

Balancing health, head, and heart helps us get into the flow state. While life's challenges don't always come from our own mistakes, the key to growth is realising that while not everything that happens is our fault, everything in our lives is our responsibility.

From Intention to Impact: Aligning Purpose, Values, and Goals through the Theory of Change

Purpose Is Not a Poster. It's the Engine.

Organisations all start with great intentions of being purpose-driven. They draft vision statements, hang values on walls, and set bold long-term goals. But unless those words actively shape decisions in the moment, guide everyday behaviours, and influence the rhythm of how business is done, they remain little more than decoration.

Purpose, when lived, is not simply an idea. It is a strategy. Purpose is what engages the heart of the team. It becomes the filter through which choices are made, people are supported, and trade-offs are navigated. Without this anchor, strategy becomes mechanical, culture becomes fragmented, and trust begins to erode.

Purpose cannot be something created in the boardroom and handed down. It cannot belong only to the executive team. Every single person in the organisation, from the most senior to the newest hire, needs to feel emotionally engaged with what the organisation stands for. That emotional connection is what builds commitment, aligns behaviours, and fuels performance.

Values Are Lived, Not Laminated

Leadership teams can confuse aspirational values with operational ones. They put words like *integrity, collaboration,* or *excellence* on the wall. Those words mean nothing if they are not demonstrated in daily decisions, conversations, and behaviours.

There is a disconnect if your values include *integrity,* but people are rewarded for short-term wins that compromise long-term trust. If your stated purpose is *empowering communities,* but all your decisions concentrate power at the top, you send the opposite message. It's not enough to say the right things. You have to live them, both internally and externally.

In every organisation, culture is shaped by what is allowed, reinforced, and ignored. And values sit at the heart of those choices.

Anyone can talk about values when times are good. The test comes when times are hard. When trade-offs are painful, deadlines are tight, and pressures mount, values become the compass. They are what we lean on to make tough decisions with clarity and integrity.

Think about a company that claims *collaboration* as a core value. The posters say it. The policies reference it. But in practice, meetings are dominated by a few voices, information is hoarded, and teams compete rather than support one another. People are promoted for protecting their turf, not for building bridges. Over time, the culture shifts quietly towards mistrust and self-preservation. Organisations fracture when values are not lived and aligned from the top down. Trust breaks down. Engagement fades. Good people leave. Strategy stalls because the culture underneath it is unstable.

On the other hand, when values are lived, something powerful happens. People feel safe, seen, and connected to something bigger than themselves. Decisions become clearer. Accountability feels purposeful, not punitive. People hold themselves and one another to a higher standard, guided by shared values and personal responsibility.

Living your values means asking, "*Does this action reflect who we say we are?*" and having the courage to change course if the answer is no. It means being consistent even when it is inconvenient. Culture is not built in one big moment, but in the small ones repeated over time. When you live your values, they become more than words. They become habits. They become culture. And culture determines whether vision becomes reality.

Case Study: When Values Built a Market Leader

I witnessed this first-hand in the very first pharmaceutical organisation I worked for. I had been at the organisation for 1.5 years before it was sold, and a new CEO, John, arrived. Over the 10 years under this new CEO's leadership, the company steadily increased its market share. Year after year, the organisation continued to grow from strength to strength.

He was a strong and decisive CEO. He demanded a lot of himself and his leadership team, set high expectations, and was authentically true to the core values. What set him apart was his vision and his commitment to living by his values every single day. He did not just speak about integrity, respect, or accountability; he demonstrated them in how he led, made decisions, and treated people.

He asked the same of his senior leadership team. Across every state and every office, values were not just laminated statements, but lived actions. People felt proud to uphold them because they were modelled from the very top. And the result? People would have gone to the trenches for him and for the organisation. It was the best period of my career, a culture where people gave their best willingly because they believed in both the purpose and the person driving it.

But when he left, and another major global player acquired the business, things changed. CEOs rotated through the organisation like a constant handover, never settling long enough to take root, and the culture began to unravel. Values that had once been non-negotiable were neglected. Toxic behaviours were tolerated at all levels. Customers were treated like numbers. Purpose and values became empty words rather than guiding principles. The only key metric that remained was the bottom line.

Today, that once-dominant company has a market share that has dwindled significantly, and while people can argue it's a sign of the times, the memories of those who lived through the earlier years remain strong. We still remember what can happen when values are genuinely lived, and the caution of what happens when they are abandoned.

How to Bring Values to Life

Living values requires consistency. They need to be embedded in the organisation's **operating rhythm**; the predictable set of routines, conversations, and practices that guide how work gets done. When values are built into the rhythm of business, they stop being abstract and start becoming habits.

1. Recruitment, Onboarding, and Promotion

- **Recruitment:** Design interview questions that test alignment with values. For example, if collaboration is a core value, ask candidates to describe a time they succeeded through teamwork rather than individual effort.
- **Onboarding:** Introduce new hires to values not as abstract principles, but as stories and case studies of how those values have guided past decisions. Invite leaders and peers to share personal examples.
- **Promotion:** Make advancement contingent on *how* results are achieved, not just what results are achieved. Recognise those who role-model values in their daily work.

In the operating rhythm: Embed values conversations into monthly hiring panels, quarterly promotion reviews, and onboarding sessions so they are always tied to people decisions.

2. Performance Reviews

- Include **behavioural indicators** of each value in review templates. For example, under integrity:

"Consistently follows through on commitments and
addresses issues directly rather than avoiding them."
- Train managers to give feedback through the lens of
  values: "This project was successful not just because of
  the result, but because of the way you lived our values of
  collaboration and accountability throughout."

In the operating rhythm: Integrate values into bi-annual or
quarterly performance reviews. Encourage managers to use weekly
one-on-ones to highlight day-to-day examples of values in action.

3. Recognition and Psychological Safety

- **Recognition:** Celebrate lived values through both
  formal (awards, newsletters, intranet shout-outs) and
  informal (verbal acknowledgment in team meetings)
  channels.
- **Accountability:** Create safe spaces where people can
  respectfully call out when behaviours are misaligned
  with values. This is not about punishment, but about
  learning and growth.

In the operating rhythm: Dedicate time in monthly team
meetings for "values in action" reflections, where staff share examples
of colleagues who demonstrated values. In quarterly town halls, highlight organisational stories where values influenced key decisions.

4. Rewards, Leadership Behaviours, and Conflict Resolution

- **Rewards:** Align bonus structures, promotions, and

recognition programs to reinforce values-driven behaviours, not just outcomes.

- **Leadership:** Ensure senior leaders are consistently role-modelling values.
- **Conflict Resolution:** Use values as a framework for resolving disagreements. Ask, *"Which of our values can guide us here?"* This shifts debates from personal positions to shared principles.

In the operating rhythm: Use values as the foundation for annual reward cycles, quarterly conflict reviews, and monthly leadership alignment sessions.

5. Co-Defining Values in Practice

Invite teams to translate each organisational value into specific, observable behaviours relevant to their work. For example:

- *Customer focus* might mean "responding to client queries within 24 hours".
  - *Respect* might mean "listening without interruption in team discussions".

This co-definition makes values real, relatable, and owned by the people who live them.

In the operating rhythm: Run quarterly workshops or retrospectives where teams reflect on whether they are living the values they defined, and update examples as the context evolves.

Putting It All Together: Values in the Operating Rhythm

- **Daily:** Leaders' role-model values in micro-interactions; how they respond to pressure, how they treat people, how they make quick decisions.
- **Weekly:** Teams highlight values in one-on-ones or huddles by recognising small wins where values guided action.
- **Monthly:** Team meetings include space for "values in action" stories, both positive and constructive.
- **Quarterly:** Formal reviews and planning sessions integrate values into performance, recognition, and strategic alignment.
- **Annually,** reward and promotion cycles explicitly evaluate how well values have been lived alongside business outcomes.

When values are embedded into the daily, weekly, monthly, quarterly, and annual rhythm of work, they stop being aspirational slogans and become the fabric of culture.

How to Bring Values to Life

- Integrate values into recruitment, onboarding, and promotion decisions.
- Include behavioural examples of values in performance reviews.
- Call out when values are being lived–and when they're not– with psychological safety.
- Align reward systems, leadership behaviours, and conflict-resolution approaches with the stated values.

- Invite teams to co-define what each value looks like in practice, making it real and relatable.

Bridging the Head and the Heart

Strategic teams know that values need to be more than slogans. They translate those values into systems, habits, and rituals that reinforce them at every level. They build KPIs around purpose, not just profit. They include behavioural criteria in performance conversations. They design team rhythms that revisit values, not just targets.

This connection between values and actions is imperative for anyone who wants to influence from the inside out. It is not soft. It is strategic. Because when people are aligned, when values are alive, and when purpose is emotionally owned, not just intellectually understood, execution becomes sharper, trust becomes deeper, and meaningful change becomes possible.

That is the power of Praxis: The integration of belief with behaviour.

The Theory of Change Strategic Framework

When values are genuinely lived, culture becomes the expression of purpose in motion. Yet alignment cannot rely on goodwill or intention alone. It needs a framework that links belief to behaviour and ensures purpose translates into measurable impact. The Theory of Change offers that framework. It helps leaders and teams stay connected to what matters.

The Theory of Change, widely used in the social impact sector, is equally powerful in organisational life. At its core, it asks one deceptively simple question:

"If we truly believe in this purpose, what should we do, consistently, to bring it to life?"

This question shifts the focus from words to action. It asks us to start at the end, with the change or legacy we want to create, and then work backwards. What needs to change? How will we know it is working? And what actions, guided by which beliefs, will get us there?

This backward-mapping approach is powerful because it creates coherence. Every step becomes intentional. Every task connects to a deeper why. It guards against action for action's sake, replacing busyness with alignment.

The Theory of Change creates a transparent chain:

- **Beliefs**: our purpose and values
- **Activities**: our decisions and behaviours
- **Outputs**: what we deliver or produce
- **Outcomes**: what changes as a result
- **Impact**: the legacy we leave

Keeping this chain visible forces honesty. It demands that organisations ask, *"Do our actions match what we say we believe? Do we behave with integrity when no one is watching? Are we building systems and structures that reinforce our values, or do they uninten-*

tionally undermine them?"

How to Put the Theory of Change Into Practice

- Develop a Theory of Change map for major projects, strategic plans, or cultural transformation efforts.
- Begin planning sessions by asking, *"What impact are we trying to create?"* and work backwards from there.
- Encourage teams to connect their daily work not just to outputs, but to outcomes and long-term impact.
- Use the model to align performance indicators, organisational objectives, and cultural behaviours, so they tell a single story.
- Review progress regularly, adjusting based on what is actually changing rather than what was intended.

When used consistently, the Theory of Change becomes more than a planning tool. It is a way of thinking, a discipline that keeps purpose, values, and behaviours aligned so that impact is intentional rather than accidental.

The Integrity of Accountability through Praxis

Praxis is the integration of belief with behaviour. It is where awareness meets action, and the Theory of Change becomes lived experience. It's also the space where ideas turn into impact through consistency, clarity, and courage. But for change to last, it needs structure. It needs accountability.

Accountability is one of the quietest and most powerful forces in leadership. It holds trust, consistency, and integrity together. Without it, strong strategies falter. With it, people know where they stand, what is expected of them, and why their work matters. Accountability is not blame or punishment. It is ownership of words, actions, and impact. It creates psychological safety without lowering standards.

When accountability lives only in systems, it feels like control. When it lives in people, it feels like respect. At its best, it is an act of honour that says, I value this enough to take responsibility for it.

Assuming accountability will appear on its own is a common mistake. It needs to be modelled, practised, and reinforced until it becomes part of a team's identity and DNA. It begins with clarity. Without clarity, effort turns into confusion. Once expectations are clear, the next step is an honest, constructive conversation. Encouraging accountability creates space for feedback and reflection. In accountable teams, people move faster because they trust one another and also know what to expect. They do not wait for permission. They rely on shared principles instead of constant oversight. That trust creates a disciplined, effective freedom.

Accountability requires courage. Courage to speak the truth when silence feels safer. Courage to acknowledge when you fell short. Courage to hold others to the same standard with compassion.

Leaders who create lasting impact do not shy away from hard conversations. They have them early and with heart. Accountability is not a weapon. It is a mirror that reflects our intentions and our integrity.

When accountability is lived rather than enforced, it becomes contagious. It builds trust, sharpens execution, and keeps purpose alive long after the meeting ends. It is not about control. It is about commitment. When commitment becomes culture, teams stop working for a leader and start working with them.

Reflection Exercise: Living Your Values, Creating Impact

Take some time to reflect on how purpose and values show up in your own context. Write your answers to the following prompts:

1. **Beliefs:** What core purpose or values do you (or your organisation) claim to stand for?
2. **Activities:** How are these values reflected in the everyday decisions you make? Where are they missing?
3. **Outputs:** What do you produce or deliver as a result of these actions?
4. **Outcomes:** What actually changes for people, clients, or communities because of those outputs?
5. **Impact:** Looking further ahead, what legacy is being created? Is it the one you intend?

Activity: Think of a difficult decision you or your organisation had to make recently.

- What values were at stake?
- Which values were upheld, and which were compromised?
- How did those choices affect trust, relationships, and outcomes?
- If you had used values as the guiding compass, what might you have done differently?
- Looking ahead, what would it look like to make the next tough decision with your values front and centre?

Keep your notes visible and revisit them regularly. Just as purpose is not a poster, reflection is not a one-time activity.

Chapter 10

Implementing S.T.O.P.
Strategic Tactical Operational Priorities

"You can never manage time. You can only manage activities."
— Reem Borrows

Time is one of those commodities we all wish we had more of. There's never enough time to get everything done. The constant pressure to be productive can lead to an overwhelming cycle of busyness, but at the end of the day, do we even know what we accomplished?

Time cannot be managed. Life moves forward whether we're ready or not.

What we *can* manage, however, are our activities, choices, focus, and how we execute the things that matter.

Two people can have the same 24 hours; one makes progress, while the other has a calendar packed with meetings, an overflowing inbox, and every task feels urgent. One calmly prioritises meaningful actions while the other jumps from one thing to the next, barely pausing to think.

These habits can begin as early as high school, when students spend hours preparing for exams by rewriting their notes, rearranging their study space, and scrolling through their phone without focusing on the key material. They've spent time and energy being busy, but when the exam comes, they realise they spent more time preparing to study than actually studying.

Someone trying to improve their health might spend hours researching workout plans, watching fitness videos, and reading about diet strategies, without ever setting foot in a gym or changing their eating habits. They've consumed information, but they haven't taken action.

The issue isn't a lack of time. It's a lack of structure around execution. Instead of focusing on high-impact activities, people get caught up in what feels urgent, what's easiest to do, or what keeps them "busy."

The Knowing-Doing Gap: Why People Don't Take Action

Most people already know what they need to do. The real challenge isn't a lack of knowledge. It's the failure to act on what they know.

This is known as the Knowing-Doing Gap. It's the space where good intentions stall, and progress is quietly put on hold.

Think about how often people set goals with genuine enthusiasm, only to find themselves in the same place weeks or months later. They've read the books, taken the courses, and made the plans. They talk about what they're going to do. Yet nothing changes.

This isn't because they don't care. It isn't because they're incapable. It's because taking action often involves discomfort. Risk, uncertainty, effort, and exposure all trigger resistance. The brain seeks familiarity and safety, even when change is clearly needed.

Instead of naming this resistance, people tell themselves they need more time, more preparation, or better circumstances. They wait for the right moment. Often, that moment never arrives.

The Knowing-Doing Gap doesn't exist only at the individual level. It shows up just as clearly in organisations. Leaders and teams attend strategy sessions, engage consultants, and build detailed action plans. Months later, very little has changed. Ideas that once felt transformative sit in slide decks and folders, untouched. The organisation knows what needs to happen, yet execution falls short.

Because organisations are made up of people, they fall into familiar routines. Teams delay decisions while waiting for certainty, better market conditions, or full agreement. They prioritise what feels safe over what is necessary. When action finally happens, it is often rushed, reactive, and pressured. Mistakes follow.

Analysis increases. Meetings multiply. More information is gathered. Planning is mistaken for progress. But no amount of planning replaces action.

Closing the Knowing-Doing Gap requires a shift in emphasis. Execution must be valued as much as strategy. This means:

- Holding people accountable for outcomes, not just ideas
- Identifying non-productive activity and replacing it with action aligned to real goals
- Encouraging movement before certainty, knowing momentum builds clarity
- Treating mistakes as feedback rather than failure

The most effective way to close the gap is not through grand gestures. It happens through small, deliberate actions. Not waiting for motivation. Not perfecting every detail. Simply taking the next tangible step.

This is where prioritisation becomes critical. When everything feels important, nothing moves. The next section introduces a practical way to decide what deserves your energy now, so action becomes possible rather than overwhelming.

Breaking It Down to the Lowest Common Denominator

One of the simplest and most powerful tools for action is breaking things down to the lowest common denominator. When we face big change, new strategies, or ambitious goals, our natural tendency is to procrastinate. The brain interprets anything that feels big as threatening. We delay, rationalise, or tell ourselves we need more time, more clarity, or more preparation.

When you take a challenge and reduce it to the smallest possible step, the dynamic changes. The brain reads it as manageable. Instead of trying to scale the whole mountain at once, you take the first step. That single, simple action creates momentum. Once momentum begins, the fear that feeds procrastination loosens its hold.

Breaking things down does not mean oversimplifying or lowering the bar. It means removing noise and unnecessary complexity so the next action feels clear and doable. You begin to focus on what actually moves things forward. For example, if a team needs to shift its culture, the lowest common denominator may be as simple as opening every meeting with one intentional question that invites real connection. Small actions like this cut through the paralysis of too much, too hard, too soon, and replace it with progress.

When this practice becomes habitual, it creates movement not only for you but for those around you. Reducing change into small, tangible steps builds confidence, ease, and a sense of possibility. What once felt overwhelming starts to feel achievable. Transformation does not arrive through dramatic gestures. It comes from consistent, simple actions repeated over time.

Momentum is the key. Action builds confidence. The more we act, the more capable we feel. And the more capable we feel, the easier it becomes to take the next step. That is why the first step often feels the hardest. Progress is created through doing, even when it feels uncomfortable.

S.T.O.P. Chasing Your Tail: A Smarter Way to Get Things Done

"You can have it all. You just can't have it all at once." - Reem

There's a common misconception that success comes from doing as much as possible, as quickly as possible. That getting ahead means juggling multiple priorities and staying in constant motion, without space to pause or reflect. Over time, this way of operating leads to exhaustion rather than real progress.

How often do we ask someone how they're doing and hear, "I'm busy"? Busyness to the point of chaos is often worn as a badge of honour, yet it is neither sustainable nor effective.

We also tend to misjudge time. We overestimate what can be achieved in a single day, packing our schedules with unrealistic expectations, while underestimating what steady, intentional effort can create over three years. Real progress rarely comes from short bursts of intensity. It comes from focus, consistency, and persistence over time.

The S.T.O.P. model supports this way of working. It creates deliberate execution by helping individuals and teams focus on what truly matters, cut through the noise, and take intentional action that moves them forward in a meaningful way.

What S.T.O.P. Stands For on Two Fronts and Why It Matters

At Dreem, the S.T.O.P. Acronyms are so central to our work that we use them on two fronts. The first is as a framework for Strategic, Tactical, and Operational Priorities, which highlights the necessity for organisations and individuals to pause and focus on long-term planning, clear priorities, and disciplined execution. The second is as a real-time decision-making tool: Stop, Think, Observe, Proceed. In moments of urgency or distraction, this version of S.T.O.P. creates the pause needed to avoid knee-jerk reactions and instead act with clarity and intention.

Both uses share the same purpose: to slow you down, create space, and align your actions with what matters most.

They also help you clearly see the gap between where you are now and where you want to be, because once that gap is visible, priorities become obvious.

S.T.O.P.: Strategic Tactical Operational Priorities - A framework designed to bring clarity, structure, and alignment to executing tasks, making decisions, and setting priorities.

The model is built around four core principles:

- *Clarify strategic objectives so every action is intentional.* Clarifying strategic objectives means defining what success looks like, both in the long term and in daily execution. It requires stepping back, identifying key outcomes, and ensuring every action serves a larger goal.
- *Eliminate distractions and inefficiencies that waste time.* Individuals and teams can critically examine which actions move the needle and eliminate everything else. It means saying no to things that don't align with strategic goals, priorities, and company values.

- *Create an operating rhythm that drives consistency.* An effective operating rhythm ensures that progress is tracked, obstacles are identified early, and momentum is maintained. Whether through weekly team check-ins, monthly strategy reviews, or a personal habit of reviewing goals each morning, an operating rhythm prioritises forward motion through consistent habits.
- *Align daily and weekly activities with the long-term vision.* Without alignment, it's easy to get stuck in short-term firefighting rather than long-term progress. S.T.O.P. ensures that daily actions are directly linked to strategic goals so that progress isn't accidental, it's intentional.

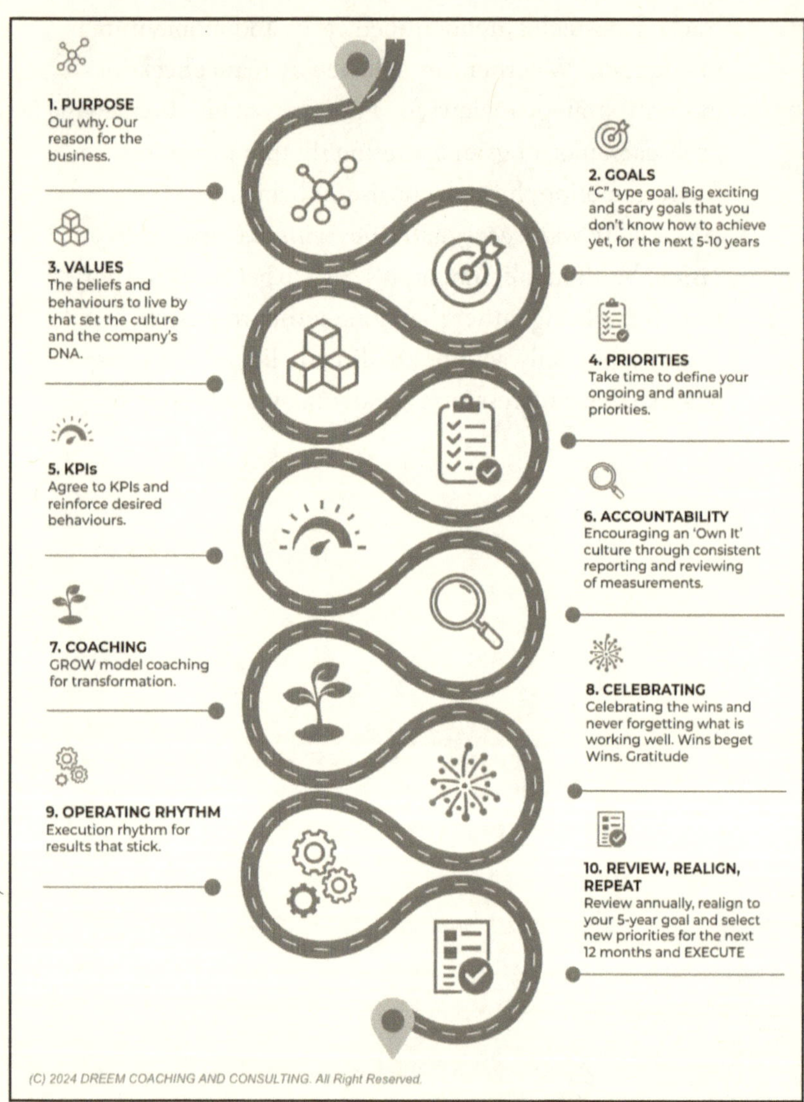

The S.T.O.P. Model. Source: Dream Coaching and Consulting PTY LTD 2020.

Dreem S.T.O.P. - Strategic Tactical Operational Priorities

S.T.O.P. - A Real-Time Decision-Making Tool

Beyond execution, S.T.O.P. also serves as a real-time decision-making framework that prevents knee-jerk reactions driven by urgency. When faced with a challenge, distraction, or new opportunity, applying S.T.O.P. helps cut through the noise and make better choices.

It follows a four-step process:

1. **Stop:** Before reacting, pause. When an issue comes up, don't react and jump into it headfirst. Before making a decision, take a moment to ensure you're not being swayed by urgency rather than importance.

2. **Think**: Step back and assess the bigger picture. Once you've paused, the next step is to evaluate the situation in the context of your broader priorities. What is the real issue? Is this aligned with your long-term objectives? Thinking before acting creates space for strategic decision-making rather than reactive problem-solving.

3. **Observe**: Identify patterns, obstacles, and opportunities. Observation is about recognising trends rather than just reacting to individual events. Is this the first time this problem has come up? Are there patterns in behaviour that need to be addressed? What are the obstacles preventing progress? Where are the opportunities to improve efficiency? By observing carefully, individuals and teams can make more informed decisions.

4. **Proceed:** Take intentional action with confidence. The final step is to **act with intention**. This means taking action that aligns with long-term goals, eliminates distractions, and maintains consistency. Proceeding with confidence isn't about knowing everything will work out

perfectly. It's about knowing the decision was made with clarity, not in reaction to external pressures.

The Impact of Applying S.T.O.P.

When we consistently apply S.T.O.P., we become strategic. We eliminate time-wasting activities, prioritise effectively, and ensure every action serves a purpose.

Applying S.T.O.P. before making decisions will lead to shorter, more productive meetings. Workloads will be aligned with priorities, rather than dictated by urgency. People will feel in control of their schedules, not overwhelmed by them.

On a personal level, applying S.T.O.P. can mean the difference between constantly feeling overwhelmed and behind and making steady, meaningful progress toward goals. S.T.O.P. helps ensure that energy is spent where it counts, in all that we do.

It is the ultimate tool to give you and your team the gift of time.

Drop the Dead Weight, Kickstart the Right Moves, and Keep the Wins Coming

Because we primarily operate on autopilot, we don't often ask ourselves, *"Is this working?"*

The *Stop, Start, Continue* framework is a simple, powerful tool that breaks this cycle. It forces our teams and us to pause, evaluate current activities, and make intentional adjustments. Instead of doing things because *"that's how we've always done it"*, we can apply *the Stop, Start, Continue* framework to ensure that time and energy are spent where they have the most impact.

The *Stop, Start, Continue* framework consists of three simple but essential steps:

- STOP: Identify activities, habits, and processes that waste time, create inefficiencies, or hold back progress.

- START: Introduce new behaviours, strategies, or processes that will drive better results.
- CONTINUE: recognise and reinforce what's already working well. Maintain consistency in areas that are delivering results.

Dreem worked with a national sales team struggling with inefficiencies, despite a strong product pipeline and talented individuals. Their revenue growth had stalled, and frustration was mounting. Together with the team, we assessed their workflow and determined that activity management was one of the biggest issues.

Each week, the sales team sat through long internal meetings that disrupted their workflow and pulled them away from revenue-generating activities. Reports were being created, but rarely used effectively. Communication felt scattered, with no structured rhythm to its execution.

To address this, we applied *Stop, Start, Continue*:

START	STOP	CONTINUE
What are things that I/we need to START doing?	What are we currently doing that I/we can or should STOP?	What am I/we doing now that works and should CONTINUE?

- STOP: We eliminated lengthy, unfocused meetings that took valuable selling time. All internal meetings required a clear agenda, and any that didn't were removed from the calendar.
- Reports that weren't being actioned were discontinued.
- Where possible, we also reduced all one-hour internal meetings to 45 minutes, with a mandatory 15-minute no-meeting rule between meetings to give people time to close the current meeting and prepare themselves for the next.
- START: We introduced structured, short daily check-ins, no more than 15 minutes, to ensure alignment without unnecessary time loss. The team also started using a shared digital dashboard to track performance in real time, reducing the need for excessive reporting. Additionally, we introduced a weekly agenda that focused on three key areas:

1. What was completed in the previous week? A quick review of accomplishments ensured that progress was being tracked and recognised.
2. What barriers were faced? This allowed salespeople to highlight obstacles that had slowed them down, whether internal (e.g., waiting on approvals) or external (e.g., client delays).
3. What barriers need to be removed to allow them to complete their tasks in the coming week? By proactively addressing potential roadblocks, managers could step in and provide support where needed, ensuring that each salesperson had the best chance of meeting their targets.

- CONTINUE: Weekly KPI tracking and recognition of wins remained in place, as this had a direct impact on motivation and performance. Celebrating progress was a key factor in maintaining momentum.

Within weeks, the sales team's changes were noticeable. They had more time to focus on selling; communication became more streamlined, and their conversion rates improved because they spent more time with clients rather than in meetings. The weekly agenda also became a game-changer, ensuring that fundamental problems were solved in real-time rather than issues piling up and causing frustration.

The Urgency Trap: Stop Putting Out Fires and Start Making Real Progress

When teams apply the Stop, Start, Continue framework, they quickly see how small adjustments can make a huge difference. However, there's another challenge that often surfaces: figuring out what to prioritise.

Even after eliminating unnecessary meetings, streamlining communication, improving processes, and introducing better execution rhythms, people still find themselves swamped with work. The issue isn't always about cutting things out. It's about knowing what to focus on first. The struggle to prioritise isn't about a lack of time. It's about how that time is spent. Many of us fall into the trap of working on what feels urgent rather than what is important. The challenge here is that urgent tasks scream the loudest, while important tasks quietly wait in the background, often until it's too late.

The Eisenhower Matrix, also known as the Urgent-Important Matrix, is another simple yet powerful tool that helps separate the noise from the real work. It offers a process to help people stop reacting and start prioritising by categorising tasks into four quadrants:

The Eisenhower Matrix

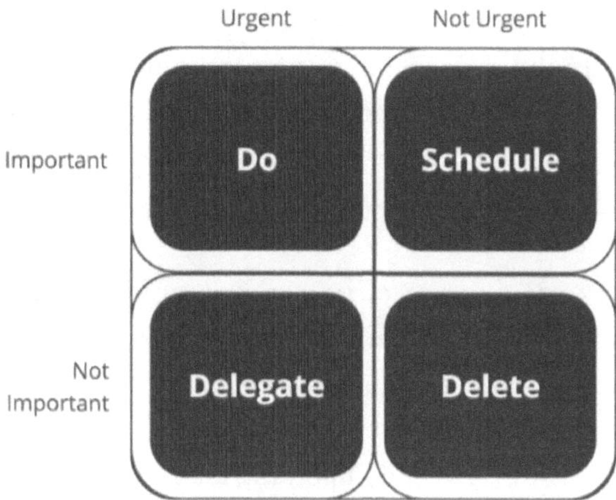

1. **Urgent & Important:** These tasks require immediate action. They often come in the form of crises, looming deadlines, or major client issues. They can't be ignored, but if everything falls into this category, it's a sign that long-term planning is being neglected.

2. **Important But Not Urgent:** This is the quadrant of strategic thinking, growth, and long-term success. It includes tasks such as planning, leadership development, relationship-building, and work that demands focus. The challenge? Because these tasks don't have an immediate deadline, they often get pushed aside for something that feels more pressing.

3. **Urgent But Not Important:** These tasks demand immediate attention but do not necessarily require your involvement. Think of low-priority emails, administrative work, minor requests, or interruptions that could be delegated. Delegating these tasks or setting clear boundaries around interruptions can free up time for more valuable work.

4. **Neither Urgent nor Important:** Mindless scrolling through emails that don't need a response, sitting in pointless meetings with no clear purpose, engaging in office politics, or spending hours refining a report that no one will ever read. Eliminating or drastically reducing time spent in this quadrant can dramatically increase productivity.

If we're not careful, many of us can bounce between urgent, low-value tasks, leaving little room for the meaningful work that drives results. The key is to shift focus to planning.

- If a task is urgent and important, tackle it immediately, but also ask, *"Could this have been prevented?"*
- If a task is important but not urgent, schedule time for it and protect that time fiercely. This step is where progress happens.
- If a task is urgent but not important, delegate it or find a way to handle it efficiently without wasting valuable energy.
- If a task is neither urgent nor important, remove it. Question why you are doing these tasks in the first place.

The sales team we worked with applied this matrix to refine their workflow after implementing STOP, START, CONTINUE. They quickly realised that urgent but low-value activities were consuming most of their time, leaving little room for the high-value activities that drove sales. By shifting their focus to important but not urgent tasks, such as proactive client engagement and strategic planning, they not only improved their results but also reduced daily stress.

Shifting from urgency to importance doesn't mean ignoring pressing demands. It implies taking control of your time rather than letting external pressures dictate it. Those who consistently prioritise important work before it becomes urgent are the ones who ultimately make the biggest impact.

THE MAGIC WORD: The Secret Ingredient That Makes Execution Stick

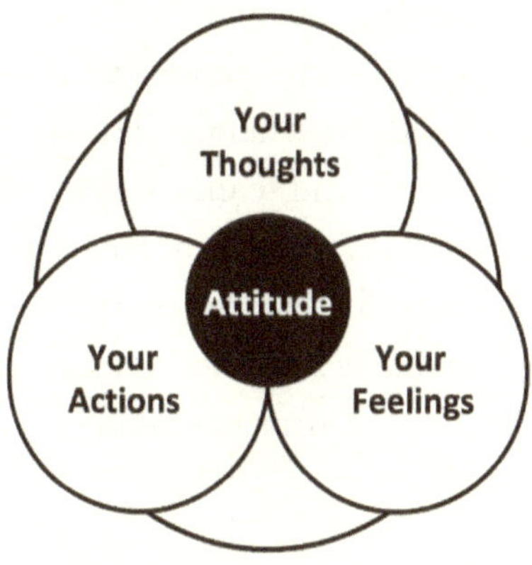

Proctor Gallagher Institute

Having the right attitude is what turns plans into action. You can have clear strategies, goals, and systems in place, but if your mindset is not right, even the best plans will fall flat.

Attitude is the composite of three parts: your thoughts, your feelings, and your actions. They work together to shape how you show up every day.

- Your thoughts guide what you believe is possible.
- Your feelings determine how motivated and engaged you are.
- Your actions turn intention into results.

If one of these is out of balance, progress slows. The key is to check in with yourself regularly.

- *What am I thinking right now?*
- *How am I feeling?*
- *Are my actions aligned with what matters most?*

Attitude is the final ingredient that brings every framework in this book to life. Attitude is not about simply showing up and being positive. It is about showing up with purpose, focus, and energy. When your thoughts, feelings, and actions work together, you create momentum, resilience, and consistency. This is when real progress happens for both individuals and teams. It gives depth to self-awareness, direction to the GROW model, heart to gratitude, and movement to emotional fluency. It determines whether the insights you gain stay as ideas or become lasting change. The right attitude transforms learning into action and turns potential into results.

Reflection Activity: Start, Stop, Continue

Take a moment to step back and reflect on your work or team performance. The Start–Stop–Continue framework is a simple yet powerful way to refocus your energy on what truly creates progress and flow.[1]

Step 1: Choose a focus area

Pick one project, process, or routine that could benefit from a reset.

Step 2: Create your three columns – Start, Stop, Continue

In each, list practical actions or habits that apply to your chosen focus.

Stop – Identify what drains time, energy, or clarity.

Ask: What's slowing us down? What no longer serves the goal?

Start – Highlight new ideas, tools, or behaviours that would create better results.

Ask: What could improve how we work, communicate, or deliver outcomes?

Continue – Recognise what's already effective and worth maintaining.

Ask: What's working well that we should preserve and strengthen?

Once complete, prioritise your list and share it with your team. Commit to one immediate action from each column. Revisit this exercise quarterly as part of your operating rhythm to stay intentional, aligned, and free from unnecessary complexity.

Clarity creates flow. This simple reflection helps you let go of what no longer serves, activate what matters most, and keep momentum alive.

Chapter 11

Escaping the Cycle

Meetings, Stagnation, and the Leadership Reset

"Unnecessary meetings are rarely a time problem. They are a leadership problem."
— *Reem Borrows*

Meetings are meant to bring people together to solve problems and make decisions. Instead, for many, they've become a productivity black hole and an endless cycle of talking about work instead of doing it.

We've covered how prioritisation, attitude, and execution fuel progress, but even the best-laid plans can be derailed by a calendar packed with meetings that could have been sorted out with an email or a quick conversation.

If your schedule looks like a wall of never-ending meetings, it's likely because somewhere along the way, meetings became a default rather than a necessity.

The issue isn't just the sheer volume of meetings, but also how they're structured. Most meetings lack a clear agenda, have too many participants, and lack defined objectives or outcomes. People show up out of obligation rather than necessity, decisions drag on over multiple sessions, and time gets eaten up discussing problems without reaching solutions. At times, meetings are called because people haven't given themselves the space to think independently.

If you've ever sat in a meeting wondering, *"Why am I even here?"*, you're not alone.

The real problem? Meetings without a purpose slow down execution. When every decision requires another meeting, momentum gets lost. When meetings don't lead to clear actions, people leave confused. And when meetings are scheduled for every minor discussion, people spend more time talking than doing.

Before scheduling a meeting, ask yourself: *Is this truly necessary?*

If the issue can be resolved with a well-structured email or a quick one-on-one conversation, skip the meeting. And if a meeting is necessary, a clear structure will ensure that it adds value rather than wasting time.

Every meeting should answer key questions:

1. What is the problem or goal? Why are we here? What needs to be solved or achieved? If this can't be clearly defined, the meeting shouldn't happen.
2. What is the current reality, and what are the options? What are the facts? Where are we now? What choices are available?
3. What are the recommendations and actions? What's the decision needed? Who is accountable for what? When will it be done?
4. Who needs to be involved and why?

If a meeting can't answer these questions, you should question why it is scheduled in the first place.

Making Meetings Work for You

Beyond better structuring meetings, people need space to do their work. Meetings should move the work forward, not replace the work itself. That means rethinking how time is allocated:

- Reduce meeting lengths – One-hour meetings are cut to 45 minutes. 30-minute meetings become 20. Most discussions don't need as much time as they're given.
- Enforce a 15-minute buffer between meetings – This space prevents people from jumping from one call to the next without time to think, reset, or process information.
- No agenda? No meeting. (Make sure the team and/or company are on board with this practice and/or committed to a *no-agenda, no-meeting* rule throughout the organisation).

The agenda only needs to include three key points:

1. Identify the aim of the meeting.
2. Clarify the current reality.
3. Outline possible solutions in order of priority.

You'll be surprised by how many meetings can be avoided once people take a moment to reflect on these three questions. By thinking them through, they often become more solution-focused and discover the answer themselves without needing a meeting.

The Productivity Hack No One Talks About

We've just unpacked how poorly structured meetings are killing execution. But even if you clean up your calendar, set clear agendas, and stop wasting hours in unproductive discussions, there's still one major problem left to solve: when do you find the time to think critically?

When was the last time you sat down, completely undisturbed, and gave yourself space to think critically? If you're like most people, the answer is probably rarely, never, or in the shower.

Most of us move from task to task, conversation to conversation, and meeting to meeting with little to no space in between. Our minds are constantly occupied and rarely clear. We're in reactive mode all day long, focusing on whatever is loudest, most urgent, or thrown at us next.

Thinking time isn't a luxury, and it's not laziness. It's a necessity. If you're not setting aside time to step back, process, and make better decisions, then you're running on autopilot. Autopilot doesn't lead to innovation, clarity, or strong execution. Instead, it leads to burnout, frustration, and wasted effort.

You don't need hours. You don't need to go on a meditation retreat.

You need 20 minutes.

Twenty minutes of uninterrupted, intentional thinking time every single day. Not while checking Slack, not while making coffee, and definitely not while sitting in yet another Zoom call.

Henry Ford, one of the greatest industrialists of his time, believed that thinking was the most valuable work a person could do. It's been reported that he set aside at least 20 minutes daily to sit silently and think. No interruptions, no distractions, just deliberate time to reflect and solve problems.

We've become addicted to *doing*. We measure productivity by the number of tasks completed rather than the quality of the decisions made. Maybe there is a reason we are called human beings, not human doers. If we don't prioritise thinking, we end up trapped in a cycle of busyness that leads nowhere. Today, most people feel guilty for sitting still. There's an assumption that *doing* is more critical than *thinking*. That if you're not busy, you're slacking off. That being in motion means you're productive.

But thinking time allows everything else to work better. It is the foundation of execution. Without it, people jump straight into doing without knowing if they're even working on the right things.

Here's how to implement thinking time into your operating rhythm:

- Schedule 20 minutes at least three times a week, if not daily, in your calendar for thinking time.
- Turn off notifications. Don't just mute them, turn them off completely. No emails, no messages, no pings pulling you away.
- Step away from your desk. Go outside, sit somewhere different, move around, and get a change of scenery from your usual workspace.
- Give yourself a question to think about. Something meaningful.
  - *What's the biggest challenge I need to solve this week?*
  - *What would success look like if I solved this problem?*
  - *What's one thing I've been avoiding that needs my attention?*
  - *What opportunities are right in front of me that I haven't noticed?*
- Work on only one question at a time.

People who build this habit start making better decisions. Overwhelm fades as they move from reacting to everything to purposefully directing their time.

And when you start thinking clearly, you begin to execute with purpose. Because once you know what needs to be done, the next step isn't about motivation. It's about discipline.

Celebrating The Grind

We glorify the outcome and downplay effort. Social media highlights the wins, the milestones, and the breakthroughs, but rarely do we see the early mornings, the quiet discipline, and the relentless consistency that made those wins possible.

We dream about success, but success is built in the grind. It doesn't happen overnight. It doesn't come from a single moment of inspiration. Success comes from sweating the small stuff, not the tasks that distract or derail us, but the details that matter and align with the goal. It is in these small, consistent actions that mastery is built, and excellence becomes second nature.

It comes from showing up every day, doing the work, and doing it well, whether you feel like it or not.

We often crave results but resist discipline. We admire athletes, musicians, and top performers without always recognising the years of deliberate practice, the countless repetitions, and the commitment to doing the small things well. When someone starts a new project, a business, or even a fitness journey, they're often motivated by the final result they want to see. They picture the promotion, the revenue, or the number on the scale. But when that result doesn't come as quickly as expected, motivation fades, frustration creeps in, and they give up.

If you commit to the action, put in the work each day, refine your skills, and make improvements, the results will naturally follow. The grind itself becomes the goal.

Execution requires consistency.

- Daily habits shape long-term outcomes.
- Repetition creates mastery - The more you do something, the more natural and automatic it becomes.
- Consistency beats motivation. Anyone can be motivated for a day. The people who succeed are the ones who keep going even when motivation fades.

We tend to see the grind as something to suffer through, something they "have to do" before they can finally enjoy success. But learn to celebrate the grind. Do not endure it. Do not push through it. Find joy in the process. Shift your perspective and start appreciating the process itself.

Gratitude for the grind isn't about pretending every day is fun or easy. It's about recognising that the hard work you put in today is shaping the person you're becoming. It's about appreciating the challenge, knowing that every small step forward is building something bigger. It's about being proud of yourself.

When you practise celebrating the grind and being present:

- You stop dreading the work and start embracing it.
- You develop resilience by understanding that every challenge is an opportunity to grow.
- You stay motivated by the process itself.

Being fully present in what you are doing, whether writing an email, engaging in a conversation, or working on a project, allows you to experience the sense of flow. The quality of your work improves. You feel more engaged, more connected, and more in control of the results you want to achieve.

Being present and celebrating the grind allows you to:

- Reduce stress. Anxiety comes from worrying about the future or regretting the past. Staying in the ***now*** brings clarity.
- Increase effectiveness. When you focus entirely on one task at a time, you perform better and more efficiently.
- Find meaning in the small things. Instead of waiting for the big win, you start to see the value in each step you take.

The Cycle Of Success: Review, Realign, And Keep Moving

Execution is moving with purpose and ensuring that your effort leads somewhere meaningful. People and organisations that keep themselves in motion without stopping to check if they're still heading in the right direction may find themselves far from the outcomes they hoped to achieve. Momentum without direction leads to exhaustion.

Getting realigned using the Dreem S.T.O.P. Review Rhythm can dramatically turn things around. A structured review cycle ensures long-term goals don't get lost and that individuals and teams stay on track, avoiding reactive chaos.

Structured reviews might feel like extra work. But progress doesn't happen automatically from grinding through each day without pausing to evaluate. A great execution strategy is like a high-performance race car. It's built for speed, precision, and results. But even the best race car in the world needs pit stops, or the engine overheats, the tyres wear down, and the whole race is over. The best drivers know they also need to pull over at strategic moments to refuel, adjust, and come back stronger.

- **The Dreem S.T.O.P. Review Rhythm** offers individuals and teams a process to operate at peak performance without burning out. Organisations need to build a structured review rhythm into their operations to maintain strategic focus and prevent the chaos of constant reactivity.

Whether we are working with a solopreneur, a CEO, a manager, a small business owner, or someone focused on career or personal growth, the starting point is always the same: creating an operating rhythm that brings clarity and steadiness to how they think, decide, and act.

- For a solopreneur, this often means replacing reactive busyness with intentional structure. Instead of responding to everything as it comes, we establish clear weekly priorities, protected thinking time, and non-negotiable moments for strategic work. The rhythm creates space to step out of day-to-day delivery and into leadership of the business itself.
- For a CEO, the rhythm creates altitude. It brings discipline to where time and attention are spent, ensuring space for strategy, people, and long-term direction. Clear executive forums, governance and decision-making cadence, and structured reflection prevent the role from being consumed by urgency, allowing the organisation to move with greater coherence and confidence.
- For a manager, the operating rhythm provides consistency in how they lead others. Regular one-to-ones, clear decision forums, and defined expectations replace ad-hoc conversations and last-minute pressure. Over time, this reduces friction, improves accountability, and shifts leadership from firefighting to intention.
- For a small business owner, the rhythm introduces focus and sustainability. It brings order to competing demands, clarifies priorities across operations, people, and growth, and reduces the reliance on constant availability. Over time, this creates consistency in decision-making and a business that can function without everything resting on one person.
- For someone focused on career or personal growth, the rhythm is more internal. It brings structure to reflection, decision-making, and habit change. Small, consistent practices replace bursts of motivation, helping build confidence, follow through on commitments, and align actions with the person they are becoming.

In every case, the operating rhythm is about creating enough structure to support clarity, balance, and sustained growth, without losing humanity or flexibility.

OPERATING RHYTHM

THE DREEM OPERATING RHYTHM ON PAGE

- **Annual Review: Defining the Big Picture**

Once a year, take a step back and define the overarching strategy, direction, and bold goals for the next 12 months. This is the big picture moment. Targets are set, but so is ensuring the entire organisation or team is aligned on where they are headed. For individuals, this annual review helps you define where you want to be a year from now and determine not what success looks like, but what needs to happen to get there.

- **Quarterly Adjustments: Course-Correcting Before It's Too Late**

Every three months, evaluate progress against strategic goals and make necessary adjustments. This check-in allows you to course-correct before small misalignments become significant problems. Teams or individuals can use these quarterly adjustments to refine tactics, eliminate what's not working, and set priorities for the next quarter.

- **Monthly Alignment: Keeping Strategy and Execution Connected**

If quarterly reviews help teams pivot, monthly reviews ensure consistent movement in the right direction. A monthly alignment, where high-level alignment meets real execution by asking, *"What projects need more attention? What bottlenecks are slowing things down? What wins should be celebrated?"* Keeping a pulse on progress ensures the strategy doesn't just sit in a document; it's translated into action.

- **Weekly Check-ins: Removing Obstacles and Sustaining Momentum**

Think of these as micro-strategy sessions, held weekly. These check-ins focus on identifying and removing obstacles, sustaining momentum, and keeping everyone accountable. Teams and individuals can reflect on what was accomplished the previous week, what challenges arose, what needs to be adjusted for the upcoming week, and what obstacles need to be removed. This is a good time to identify bottlenecks and where the workflow is being halted. These meetings should be short, intentionally focused, and purposeful, so every team member is clear on their role in driving execution.

- **Daily Execution: Small Wins, Big Impact**

Without daily action, strategies find themselves in the graveyard. Individuals focus on high-impact activities that align with their larger goals daily to avoid stalling. The key is to start the day with intention, prioritising tasks that move the needle rather than getting lost in busyness.

The Real Difference Between Growth and Stagnation

When people and teams commit to an organised working rhythm, they build energy that is sustainable over time. They move away from a "feast or famine" approach to action, where bursts of effort are followed by burnout, disengagement, or loss of momentum.

Without the Dreem S.T.O.P. rhythm, businesses often lack a simple process to step out of reaction loops. They find themselves constantly putting out fires rather than creating space to think, plan, and move forward with intention.

Progress is not about how fast you go or how much you do. It is shaped by how often you pause, review, realign, and gently refine your direction. Whether you are running a business, leading a team, or working toward personal goals, growth comes from consistent course correction rather than constant acceleration.

If you are still reading, you are already doing something many people avoid. You are slowing down enough to think, reflect, and take responsibility for how you choose to move forward. This work is not about pressure or perfection. It is about awareness, choice, and steady improvement over time.

Now it becomes less about doing more and more about deciding what matters. Where you place your time, energy, and influence shapes your experience of work and leadership. Take a breath. There is no rush. This is an invitation, not a demand.

I hope what you have read about the Dreem S.T.O.P. Framework encourages you to experiment with it in a way that feels supportive rather than heavy. Think of it as a rhythm to return to, not a system to master. A simple structure that gives you back time, space, and clarity.

To support you, I'm offering this as a gift.

Go to dreem.com.au/lead-differently to download the Dreem S.T.O.P. document. This workbook brings together the templates, reflection questions, and agendas referenced throughout this book, along with additional resources to help you apply the ideas in a practical and grounded way. Our hope at Dreem is that you use it to turn insight into action, at your own pace.

Use it on your own, with your team, or across your organisation. Treat it as a reset, or simply the next small step forward.

Work with less worry. Do better work. Lead with clarity. Focus on what truly matters as you bring your purpose to life.

That is what the Dreem S.T.O.P. offers.

The gift of time.

Reflective Exercise

1. Audit Your Meetings

- At the end of the week, review all meetings you attended.
- Ask, *"Which had a clear agenda? Which could have been an email or a quick chat? Which led to decisions or actions?"*
- Action: Identify two recurring meetings to remove, shorten, or redesign next week.

2. Block Daily Thinking Time

- Schedule 20 minutes each day for uninterrupted reflection.[1]
- Ask, *"What's one problem I'd like to solve or one idea I could explore today?"*
- Action: Capture two or three insights or actions by week's end.

3. Redefine Meeting Purpose

- Before your next meeting, clarify:
- *What's the goal or problem to solve?*
- *What are the current realities and options?*
- *What decision or action will come out of it?*
- Action: Cancel or reframe meetings that don't meet these criteria.

4. Create Space Between Tasks

- Build a 15-minute buffer after meetings to reset, capture key actions, and refocus.
- Action: Track your energy and clarity: notice how much more intentional your day feels.

5. Reframe the Grind

- Pick one repetitive or frustrating task and shift how you see it.
- Ask, *"How is this helping me grow in consistency, focus, or resilience?"*
- Action: Write one daily sentence about how this task is shaping you.

Conclusion

This isn't the End, it's the Real Beginning.

Congratulations on reaching the end of this book. If you've truly taken it in, you'll know this isn't the finish line. It's the moment before lift-off. The point where awareness becomes action and leadership becomes a lived reality.

The Health, Head, and Heart framework is a way of being a guide to leading with clarity, courage, and compassion. When you live it, you change how you lead and how you show up in the world.

When the heart leads, and the head supports, something extraordinary happens. You start choosing to serve and stop striving to prove. You begin creating energy. You become the calm in the chaos and the spark that helps others see what's possible.

Where You Go from Here

The world needs more leaders with presence. Leaders who listen before they speak, who lift others as they rise, and who stay grounded when the noise gets loud.

Lead with intention. Speak with clarity. Act with courage.

Remember, courage is not the absence of fear. It is acknowledging the fear and doing it anyway.[1]

Be the person who reminds others that strength and compassion can coexist, that focus and flow can live side by side.

Each choice you make from here shapes the culture you create, the energy you bring, and the legacy you leave behind.

This is the moment to take everything you've read and make it real. To let your actions reflect what you now know to be true. So, take the next step with purpose. Let your actions spring from authenticity and meaning, and let your leadership be reflected in how you serve, heal, and inspire.

Your greatest impact comes from who you become in the process of what you do.

Continue the Journey

Before you go, visit **dreem.com.au/lead-differently** to access three exclusive free resources designed to help you live what you've learned:

- **The Dreem GROW Coaching Framework** to empower meaningful conversations and growth.
- **The Dreem S.T.O.P. Workbook** with templates, tools, and reflection prompts to help you turn insight into action.
- **Gloria Rees' Insights e-book** is a brilliant guide to human behaviour, communication, and self-awareness.[2]

These tools are your next step toward leading with balance, focus, and flow.

And if this book has inspired you, stay connected. Follow **Dreem Coaching and Consulting** on **LinkedIn,**

Instagram, and Facebook for ongoing reflections, tools, and stories that keep this work alive in your daily leadership practice.

Leadership doesn't end when the book closes. It begins with what you do next.

About the Author

Reem Borrows is a leadership consultant, coach, keynote speaker, and author who brings together the powerful intersection of business strategy, emotional intelligence, and social impact. With over two and a half decades of experience in senior leadership roles across Sales, Marketing, and Training, Reem is known for her ability to help people and organisations unlock transformation, from the inside out.

What sets Reem apart isn't just her track record. It's her *presence*. Her work is built on the belief that leadership is not about hierarchy, it's about humanity.

She is the founder and director of Dreem Coaching and Consulting. Reem holds a Bachelor of Commerce and a Postgraduate Diploma in Strategic Human Resources and Industrial Relations. She is a graduate of the Australian Institute of Company Directors. A fierce advocate for justice, equity, and human dignity, Reem is deeply committed to elevating conversations that spark understanding, connection, and transformation across communities and cultures. She believes in the power of leadership, not only to shift companies, but to shift consciousness.

At the core of all her work is one unshakable belief: The way we lead ourselves is the way we shape the world around us.

www.dreem.com.au

Connect with Reem on social channels. Follow her on Goodreads and read her other titles.

linkedin.com/company/dreem-consulting

instagram.com/dreemcoachingandconsulting

facebook.com/dreemcoachingandconsulting

goodreads.com/Reem_Borrows

amazon.com/author/Reem-Borrows

Acknowledgments

Writing this book has been one of the most vulnerable, challenging, and soul-expanding journeys of my life, because of what it revealed in me. I set out to write a book about leadership several years ago. I was already deep into Chapter Four, exploring the frameworks, the human behaviours, and the patterns that shape how we lead. But somewhere along the way, a more profound message began to stir. As I wrote about truth, courage, and showing up with heart, my own heart began to speak louder.

It cracked open, professionally, personally, politically, and spiritually.

And that's when the second book, *From the River to the Sea: Humanizing Freedom*, was born and published at the end of 2023. It was not part of the plan. But it became clear that I couldn't continue writing about leadership until I followed the call to speak up for something even more raw and urgent: the deep longing for justice, humanity, and dignity for all people.

So, I paused this manuscript, never abandoning it, to honour the truth rising through me. That second book poured out of me like fire, grief, and love all at once. It had to come first.

And yet, this book... This book never left. It waited patiently because this was always meant to be the foundation, the container for what it means to lead not only others but also ourselves through uncertainty, conflict, complexity, and change.

And it would not have been possible without the people who have held, stretched, and walked with me every step of the way.

To my beautiful family, thank you for being my anchor, my compass, and my why. Your deep love and belief in me created the space for this book to emerge. You've reminded me that leadership isn't about power or performance, it's about presence, compassion, and courage in everyday moments.

To the clients, teams, and leaders I've had the privilege of working with over the years, thank you for your honesty, your stories, your courage, and your willingness to do the inner work. You've been my greatest teacher. The insights in this book were shaped in the trenches, in honest conversations, under absolute pressure, and through fundamental transformation. You've shown me what it means to lead with both head and heart.

To my mentors, thank you for seeing something in me before I could see it in myself. Your guidance helped shape the leader I continue to grow into.

To my business partner and dear friend of 26 years, thank you for being a constant source of wisdom, loyalty, and truth. You've seen me at my best and at my most uncertain, and through it all, you've always reflected my strength, even when I momentarily forgot it. Our friendship is rare, and our work together has only deepened that bond. Thank you for walking beside me through every season, personally and professionally.

To my mastermind group, the three of you who stood by me week in and week out, thank you. Through nearly two years of global unrest and heartache, you held space for me without question and supported me in every way. Your presence has been a steady reminder that even in the most challenging times, leadership begins with community.

To the younger version of me, the girl who often felt too much, too bold, too different, this book is for you. For the dreams you carried in silence, the questions you never stopped asking, and the fire in your belly that refused to dim. You didn't shrink; you rose.

To my beloved community and incredible friends, the activists, the truth-tellers, the bridge-builders, and those who refuse to stay silent in the face of injustice, this book carries your heartbeat. You've taught me that leadership isn't just about business or titles. It's about humanity. About standing firm in our values, even when the ground is shaking. In the depths of darkness, grief, loss, rage, and resistance, together we found something more powerful than fear: light, love, and each other.

I am nowhere near perfect. I've made plenty of mistakes in business, leadership, love, and life. Since 2023, I have been forced to look directly at my ego, my blind spots, and the places I had been operating unconsciously. Through deep pain and disbelief, my awareness cracked wide open. I've grown more in these months than I have in years.

I've come to understand how fragile the human mind really is, unless we allow the heart to lead and the mind to serve. That simple reversal changed everything for me.

And perhaps most importantly, through it all, I've learned to be gentler with myself and with others. To hold space without judgment. To soften without losing strength. To stop chasing perfection and start embracing presence.

To you, the reader, thank you. For being here. For choosing to lead with intention. For being willing to look inward so you can lead outward. I hope that these words don't just give you tools; they give you *permission*. To take up space. To walk with humility. To rise with clarity and care. And to know you're never leading alone. We don't need perfect leaders. We need present ones. And I'm honoured to walk this path beside you.

RED THREAD BOOKS

About the Publisher

Red Thread Publishing is an award-winning indie press dedicated to amplifying powerful, authentic nonfiction voices. In our first six years, we've published more than 75 books, supported over 400 authors from 32 countries, and celebrated 55 book awards, proof of the impact and quality behind every title we produce.

Our passionate team is committed to guiding authors through every step of the writing and publishing journey so their stories not only get published but make a lasting impact.

Visit *www.redthreadbooks.com*

Email us *info@redthreadbooks.com*

 instagram.com/redthreadbooks

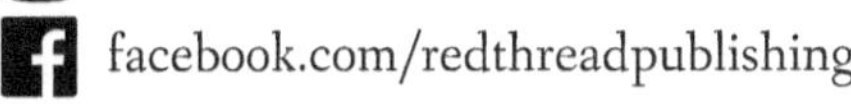 facebook.com/redthreadpublishing

Notes

Introduction

1. Twain, M. (1923). *Mark Twain's Speeches*. Harper & Brothers.
2. 7 Gallup Workplace Insights: What We Learned in 2021. (2022, January 1). *Gallup.*
3. Proctor, B. (2015). The ABCs of Success by Bob Proctor, Business & Personal Finance. A 3-Step Plan for Achieving Your Ideal Goal. https://rack.sbhealthsource.org/public/9532I4037_the_abcs_of_success_by_bob_proctor.html
4. State of the Global Workplace. (2024). GALLUP. https://www.gallup.com/workplace/349484/state-of-the-global-workplace.aspx

1. Beyond Survival

1. Maslow, A. H. (1943). A theory of human motivation. *Psychological Review,* 50(4), 370–396.
2. Deci, E. L., & Ryan, R. M. (2000). *The "what" and "why" of goal pursuits: Human needs and the self-determination of behavior.* Psychological Inquiry, 11(4), 227–268.
3. Dr Joseph Dispenza- 'What the Bleep! - Down the Rabbit Hole' (2006)
4. *Proctor, B. (2013, March). Introducing the Stick Person. Bob Proctor Lessons. https://bobproctorlessons.blogspot.com/2013/03/introducing-stick-person.html*
5. Issa, M. (2022, February 19). How Bob Proctor changed the way I thought about thoughts. Medium. https://mo-issa.medium.com/how-bob-proctor-changed-the-way-i-thought-about-thoughts-4acdb713edf
6. Luskin, F. (2003). *Forgive for Good: A Proven Prescription for Health and Happiness.* HarperOne.

2. Leading Your Health, Head, and Heart

1. Aristotle. *Metaphysics.* (Traditional).
2. Lmft, E. M. (2024, August 30). Why do you blame yourself for everything - therapy in a nutshell. Therapy in a Nutshell. https://therapyinanutshell.com/why-you-blame-yourself-for-everything/
3. Follett, M. P. (1924). *Creative Experience.* Longmans, Green and Co.

3. Mission (Very) Possible

1. Shaw, G. B. (1903). *Man and Superman*. Archibald Constable & Co.
2. Reiner, A. (1990). An Explanation of behaviour: The Triune Brain in Evolution . Role in Paleocerebral Functions. Paul D. MacLean. Plenum, New York, 1990. xxiv, 672 pp., illus. $75. Science, 250(4978), 303–305. https://doi.org/10.1126/science.250.4978.303.bhow
3. Flavell, J. H. (1963). The developmental psychology of Jean Piaget. In D Van Nostrand eBooks. https://doi.org/10.1037/11449-000
4. Ap. (2020, November 3). Why freedom demands responsibility. Wise & Shine. https://wiseandshinezine.com/2020/11/03/why-freedom-demands-responsibility/
5. Comaford, C. (2012, April 4). Got inner peace? 5 ways to get it now. Forbes. https://www.forbes.com/sites/christinecomaford/2012/04/04/got-inner-peace-5-ways-to-get-it-now/
6. Andrews, A. (2009). The Noticer: Sometimes, all a person needs is a little perspective. https://ci.nii.ac.jp/ncid/BB0660556X
7. Pritchett, P. (1994). *You2: A High Velocity Formula for Multiplying Your Personal Effectiveness in Quantum Leaps*. Pritchett & Associates.

4. The Integrative Approach

1. Lindgren, G. (2005). *Gerry Lindgren's Book on Running*.
2. Candor, R. (2023, October 2). How to avoid the problem-solving trap | Radical candor. Radical Candor. https://www.radicalcandor.com/blog/problem-solving-skills/
3. Admin. (2023, October 24). Why decision-making is an emotional intelligence skill. Lisa D. Foster, Leadership Coaching & Training. https://lisadfostercoach.com/2022/09/28/why-decision-making-is-an-emotional-intelligence-skill/

5. The Iceberg of Leadership

1. Mazhura, M. (2014). *Self-Steer: The 7-Step Playbook for Fueling Your Career*.
2. Lmft, E. M. (2024, August 30). Why do you blame yourself for everything - therapy in a nutshell. Therapy in a Nutshell. https://therapyinanutshell.com/why-you-blame-yourself-for-everything/
3. Proctor Gallagher Institute. (2010). *Thinking into Results*.
4. Fleet, T. (1934). *Concept Therapy*. Concept Therapy Institute.

6. The Courage to Lead

1. Maxwell, J. C. (2010). *The 21 Irrefutable Laws of Leadership*. Thomas Nelson.

7. Gratitude

1. Caddy, E. (1987). *The Dawn of Change*. Findhorn Press.
2. Baumeister, R. F., Bratslavsky, E., Finkenauer, C., & Vohs, K. D. (2001). Bad is stronger than good. *Review of General Psychology*, 5(4), 323–370.

8. Knowing Yourself and Understanding Others

1. Jung, C. G. (1951). *Aion: Researches into the Phenomenology of the Self*.
2. Mitchell, A. (2023, October 23). Insights colors: Understand your behavioural preferences—Juicing the Lemon. Juicing the Lemon | Insights Discovery Workshops. https://www.juicingthelemon.com/insights-colours/
3. Mitchell, A. (2023, October 23). Insights colors: Understand your behavioural preferences—Juicing the Lemon. Juicing the Lemon | Insights Discovery Workshops. https://www.juicingthelemon.com/insights-colours/

9. Leading with Flow

1. Tolle, E. (2005). *A New Earth: Awakening to Your Life's Purpose*. Penguin Books.
2. Csikszentmihalyi, M. (1990). *Flow: The Psychology of Optimal Experience*. Harper & Row.

10. Implementing S.T.O.P.

1. Daniels, P. (1970). Start-Stop-Continue: A simple tool for team feedback and improvement.

11. Escaping the Cycle

1. Newport, C. (2016). Deep Work: Rules for Focused Success in a Distracted World. Grand Central Publishing.

Conclusion

1. Redmoon, A. (1991). No Such Thing as Fear.
2. Rees, G. (2023). Insights: A Guide to Human Behaviour and Self-Awareness. Dreem Coaching and Consulting.